Community Interventions to Create Change in Children

Community Interventions to Create Change in Children has been co-published simultaneously as *Journal of Prevention & Intervention in the Community*, Volume 24, Number 2 2002.

Community Interventions to Create Change in Children

Lorna H. London, PhD
Editor

Community Interventions to Create Change in Children has been co-published simultaneously as *Journal of Prevention & Intervention in the Community*, Volume 24, Number 2 2002.

LONDON AND NEW YORK

Community Interventions to Create Change in Children has been co-published simultaneously as *Journal of Prevention & Intervention in the Community*™, Volume 24, Number 2 2002.

First published 2002 by The Haworth Press, Inc.
Published by Routledge
2 Park Square, Milton Park, Abingdon, Oxon OX14 4RN
711 Third Avenue, New York, NY 10017, USA

Routledge is an imprint of the Taylor & Francis Group, an informa business

© 2002 by The Haworth Press, Inc. All rights reserved. No part of this work may be reproduced or utilized in any form or by any means, electronic or mechanical, including photocopying, microfilm and recording, or by any information storage and retrieval system, without permission in writing from the publisher.

Cover design by Marylouise Doyle

Library of Congress Cataloging-in-Publication Data

Community interventions to create change in children / Lorna London, editor.
    p. cm.
"Co-published simultaneously as Journal of prevention & intervention in the community, volume 24, number 2, 2002."
Includes bibliographical references and index.
   ISBN 978-0-789-01991-2 (pbk)
   1. Social work with children. 2. Prejudices in children–Prevention. 3. Violence in children–Prevention. 4. Violence in adolescence–Prevention. 5. Juvenile delinquency–Prevention. I. London, Lorna. II. Journal of prevention & intervention in the community.
   HV713 .C66 2002
   362.7–dc21

2002011825

ABOUT THE EDITOR

Lorna H. London, PhD, is Assistant Professor in the Department of Leadership, Foundations, and Counseling Psychology at Loyola University in Chicago. She received her doctorate degree in clinical community psychology from the University of South Carolina. Dr. London assisted in the development and implementation of the Kids' College, a program funded by a grant from the Chicago Public Schools and designed to promote positive race relations among children. She is a member of the American Psychological Association and of the Society for Community Research and Action, a division of the APA, and serves as Chairperson of the Racial and Cultural Affairs Committee for SCRA.

Community Interventions to Create Change in Children

CONTENTS

Introduction   1

Life Imitates (and Informs) Meta-Analysis: A Participatory Approach to Increasing Understanding of Effective Youth Mentoring Practices   3
   David DuBois

Evaluation of an Incentive System at a Summer Camp for Youth Experiencing Homelessness   17
   Laura A. Nabors
   Annie Hines
   Laura Monnier

Prevention of Victimization: *Survival Skills* for Urban Youth   33
   Elena Mikalsen
   John P. Vincent
   Gerald E. Harris

Urban Children's Video Production and Performance-Based Programming: Implications for Learning and Cross-Cultural Friendships   45
   Laura Knight Lynn
   Carol Harding
   Bijai Rai
   Stephen McManus
   Kenzie Kitcharoen
   Lisa Sweatt

Kids' College: Enhancing Children's Appreciation
and Acceptance of Cultural Diversity 63
Lorna H. London
Gregory Tierney
Larisa Buhin
Dawn M. Greco
Christofer J. Cooper

Index 79

Introduction

This volume is devoted to interventions that help to make a difference in the lives of children. When working with children, it is often easiest and most convenient to reach them in the place where they spend a significant portion of their days–their schools. Our country's elementary and high schools are places for children to expand their horizons and develop the necessary academic and social skills necessary for success in this world. However, children also have many other challenges facing them, some of which cannot be addressed effectively during the school day. The role of community psychologists has become increasingly important in helping to meet the social and emotional needs of children.

In this collection, you will see how psychologists work within the community to effect positive change in the lives of children. The articles included herein shows varied interventions, methodologies and practices with diverse groups of children. The first article, by DuBois, presents commentary that highlights effective mentoring practices with children and poignantly uses a case example to illustrate a best practice approach. Secondly, a traditional behavioral reinforcement approach is implemented in a non-traditional setting. Nabors, Hines, and Monnier chronicle the use of incentives in reinforcing positive behaviors with a group of children that are often overlooked in the literature–homeless children. Thirdly, at a time where children are often teased for being different, "Prevention of Victimization: *Survival Skills* for Urban Youth" speaks to a program in which facilitators take to community parks to meet with teenagers to work on coping skills to reduce violent behaviors. The final two articles use different approaches within the community to foster positive relationships between children. In an age where technology is used to enhance learning in the classroom, Lynn and her colleagues used qualitative and quantitative methodology to explore the

---

[Haworth co-indexing entry note]: "Introduction." London, Lorna H. Co-published simultaneously in *Journal of Prevention & Intervention in the Community* (The Haworth Press, Inc.) Vol. 24, No. 2, 2002, pp. 1-2; and: *Community Interventions to Create Change in Children* (ed: Lorna H. London) The Haworth Press, Inc., 2002, pp. 1-2. Single or multiple copies of this article are available for a fee from The Haworth Document Delivery Service [1-800-HAWORTH, 9:00 a.m. - 5:00 p.m. (EST). E-mail address: getinfo@haworthpressinc.com].

© 2002 by The Haworth Press, Inc. All rights reserved.

use of video and performance-based experiences and the role that collaboration plays in the facilitation of cross-cultural friendships. Finally, in a time where there continues to be bias-motivated aggression, a group of colleagues and I are pleased to share a description of our program that is designed to reduce prejudicial attitudes and behaviors in children.

The aim of this volume is to highlight some of the many ways in which psychologists are working within the community to prevent problems and promote healthy functioning. Given that children represent our hope for the future, it is hoped that these articles guide readers to find ways to make positive changes in some meaningful ways.

Lorna H. London

Life Imitates (and Informs) Meta-Analysis: A Participatory Approach to Increasing Understanding of Effective Youth Mentoring Practices

David DuBois

University of Missouri-Columbia

SUMMARY. Mentoring programs for youth have become immensely popular in recent years. Evaluations of their effectiveness, however, have yielded mixed results. These findings underscore a need for more careful and in-depth scrutiny of programmatic features that are necessary for mentoring relationships to provide intended benefits to youth. Utilizing a novel, participatory research perspective, this paper considers the author's own experiences as a mentor of a 9-year-old boy and their relation to a set of program best practices identified in a recent meta-analysis of the literature (DuBois, Holloway, Valentine, & Cooper, in press). A framework for efforts to enhance mentoring program effectiveness is described. *[Article copies available for a fee from The Haworth Document Delivery Service: 1-800-HAWORTH. E-mail address: <getinfo@haworthpressinc.com> Website: <http://www.HaworthPress.com> © 2002 by The Haworth Press, Inc. All rights reserved.]*

Address correspondence to: David L. DuBois, 210 McAlester Hall, Department of Psychology, University of Missouri-Columbia, Columbia, MO 65211 (E-mail: DuBoisD@missouri.edu).

[Haworth co-indexing entry note]: "Life Imitates (and Informs) Meta-Analysis: A Participatory Approach to Increasing Understanding of Effective Youth Mentoring Practices." DuBois, David. Co-published simultaneously in *Journal of Prevention & Intervention in the Community* (The Haworth Press, Inc.) Vol. 24, No. 2, 2002, pp. 3-15; and: *Community Interventions to Create Change in Children* (ed: Lorna H. London) The Haworth Press, Inc., 2002, pp. 3-15. Single or multiple copies of this article are available for a fee from The Haworth Document Delivery Service [1-800-HAWORTH, 9:00 a.m. - 5:00 p.m. (EST). E-mail address: getinfo@haworthpressinc.com].

KEYWORDS. Mentoring, participatory research, prevention, program evaluation

Youth mentoring programs are a bona fide phenomenon in present day society. At latest estimate, more than 5,000 such programs are in operation in the United States (Rhodes, in press). Growth in the mentoring movement has been sparked in part by a wide array of grassroots initiatives at the state and local level and in part by powerful strategic alliances backing mentoring that have been formed between not-for-profit organizations, corporations, and politicians at a national level. All told, impressive progress is being made toward reaching the ambitious, but laudable, goal included in General Colin Powell's America's Promise Campaign, that the lives of all youth in our country should be strengthened and enriched by an ongoing relationship with at least one mentor or other caring adult (America's Promise: The Alliance for Youth, 1999).

A recurring concern voiced in the scholarly literature on youth mentoring programs, however, is that beliefs about their effectiveness used to fuel program dissemination often have been based more on evocative testimonials than "hard" scientific data (Freedman, 1992; Rhodes, 1994, in press). In this respect, the mentoring movement has at times resembled to some critics a fallacious, but often persuasive, appeal to quantity over quality. By following this line of thinking, there is the risk of devoting a substantial portion of scarce resources to a type of intervention that could prove to be less beneficial than available alternatives (Rhodes, in press). Of equal concern is that valuable opportunities may be missed to identify "best practices" within mentoring programs (National Mentoring Working Group, 1991). Once identified, these might serve to increase the likelihood of positive benefits being received by youth who participate in programs. They also could help to avoid unintended negative outcomes that have been observed when relationships fail to live up to program expectations (Grossman & Rhodes, in press).

META-ANALYSIS OF YOUTH MENTORING LITERATURE

As part of the effort to provide a stronger research foundation for mentoring initiatives, my colleagues and I recently completed a meta-analysis of existing evaluations of their effectiveness. Based on a synthesis of results of 55 studies located in the literature, we found evidence of only *modest* or *small* benefits to adjustment for the average youth participating in a mentoring program (DuBois, Holloway, Valentine, & Cooper, in press). This was true regardless of whether considering benefits in the areas of emotional or psychological well-being (e.g., self-esteem), problem or high-risk behavior (e.g., substance use), social competence, or academic performance. More substantial benefits were apparent, however, for programs that engaged in greater numbers of "best practices" (see Table 1). Our analyses in this area utilized both: (a) a theory-based index of 11 practices emphasized previously in the mentoring literature and (b) an empirically-based index comprised of 7 program characteristics that individually were found in the meta-analysis to predict stronger outcomes (see Table 1).

A subset of nine studies also compared outcomes for youth *within* programs whose relationships with mentors differed on various indicators of intensity and quality. Youth identified as having enjoyed relatively stronger mentoring relationships were found to consistently fare better on outcome measures. Greater benefits also were found for programs that target youth experiencing various forms of environmental disadvantage (e.g., poverty). By contrast, outcomes for youth exhibiting personal vulnerabilities, such as at-risk behavior, emotional prob-

TABLE 1. Mentoring Program "Best Practices"

Practice	Theory-Based	Empirically-Based
Monitoring of Program Implementation	X	X
Setting for Mentoring Activities[a]		X
Screening of Prospective Mentors	X	
Mentor Background: Helping Role or Profession		X
Mentor/Youth Matching	X	
Mentor Pre-Match Training	X	
Expectations: Frequency of Contact	X	X
Expectations: Length of Relationship	X	
Supervision	X	
Ongoing Training	X	X
Mentor Support Group	X	
Structured Activities for Mentors and Youth	X	X
Parent Support/Involvement	X	X

Note. Based on findings from a meta-analysis of the effectiveness of youth mentoring programs (DuBois et al., in press).
[a] Programs in community and other settings outside of school (e.g., workplace) yielded the most favorable outcomes.

lems, or academic difficulties, were notably less positive. In fact, for programs that failed to adhere to a majority of the designated best practices, findings were in the direction of mentoring having had a negative or harmful influence on vulnerable youth (DuBois et al., in press).

Cumulatively, our findings underscore the reality that simply pairing a mentor with youth in a program is no guarantee of positive results or benefits (Freedman, 1992; Rhodes, in press). Outcomes clearly vary substantially both across and within programs. It appears, moreover, that these often amount to benefits that are so small to be of questionable practical significance. As noted, in some instances there is evidence of unintended negative effects as well. From a more encouraging perspective, available findings serve to delineate several interrelated sets of factors that appear important to take into account in efforts to enhance the effectiveness of mentoring programs for youth. These include salient features of programs (i.e., "best practices"), characteristics of the relationships formed between individual youth and mentors within programs, and the personal and environmental backgrounds of the youth who are targeted to receive mentoring.

PARTICIPATORY RESEARCH AND YOUTH MENTORING

Traditionally, a premium has been placed in empirical research on objectivity, such as in the types of measures employed, data analytic procedures used, and so forth. This view is typically extended to the investigator himself or herself, who ideally should not have a direct personal involvement or association with the settings or persons being researched. Meta-analysis could be cited as a prime exemplar of these principles. It involves the use of objective methods to evaluate findings from multiple studies conducted by others (Cooper, 1998). Accordingly, it eliminates risk for bias due to over-interpretation of the results of a single study as well as that which may arise from personal investment of researchers in data they themselves have collected.

Yet, increasingly, there is recognition of the costs or limitations that may be associated with exclusive reliance on traditional, quantitatively-oriented research methodologies. A recurring theme is that qualitative methods of inquiry can and should be used to complement quantitative approaches (Banyard & Miller, 1998). One specific area of growing interest in recent years has been *participatory research* methods (Brydon-Miller & Tolman, 2001). These methods extend traditional qualitative approaches, such as ethnographic field observation, in several ways. One of these is to allow for a role of the researcher as a direct participant in and agent of interaction with the phenomena under study. A basic tenet underlying participatory approaches is that there are multiple ways or routes to understanding and knowledge. Notably, these are assumed to include the researcher's own subjective interpretations and insights derived through direct personal experience with the issues under investigation (Brydon-Miller & Tolman, 2001). As a result, it is argued that traditional positivistic methods, despite being the dominant model of science, are not without viable alternatives that incorporate a less neutral and more involved stance of the investigator.

Several considerations suggest that participatory research methods could be useful for increasing understanding and appreciation of processes and outcomes in youth mentoring programs. Mentors and youth in community-based mentoring programs such as Big Brother/Big Sisters (BB/BS) typically are given wide latitude to choose when and how they will spend time together. In addition, many of their interactions are likely to take place in settings not readily accessible to outside observation (e.g., home of the mentor or youth). A participatory approach thus represents an opportunity for the researcher to gain relatively extensive and firsthand knowledge of facets of mentoring relationships that might otherwise be difficult to access using more traditional methodologies.

In addition, mentoring relationships formed through programs such as BB/BS are not time-limited and in many instances may continue for several years. In this regard, participatory involvement in a mentoring relationship may afford the opportunity to observe how relationships and their effects on youth unfold over extended periods of time. To date, very few quantitative evaluations of programs have provided this type of information (DuBois et al., in press).

With these considerations in mind, the following section of this paper provides a description of the author's experiences as a mentor for a youth over a 15-month period in a BB/BS program. Arguably, the meta-analytic synthesis referred to previously and an N of 1 case study are positioned very close to the opposite end points of the quantitative-qualitative continuum. Nevertheless, the focus will be on illustrating the potential for the two modes of inquiry to complement and mutually inform one another with respect to enhancing understanding of factors affecting mentoring program effectiveness. Three primary questions guide the analysis:

1. To what extent and in what ways are the author's observations as a mentor consistent with major trends evident in findings of

empirical studies as delineated in results and conclusions of the meta-analysis?
2. In what ways do the author's experiences as a mentor help to deepen understanding of processes that may be important in accounting for previously reported findings?
3. In what ways do impressions formed by the author in his role as a mentor serve to highlight issues or concerns that have not received significant attention in prior research?

Space constraints preclude an exhaustive analysis of all aspects of the author's experiences relevant to these questions. The aim instead will be to discuss exemplars of pertinent observations and insights and their relations to existing empirical findings in the literature. The analysis provided then will be used as a basis to suggest a general conceptual framework for enhancing mentoring program effectiveness. A key goal in doing so will be to illustrate the potential value of combining insights gleaned from even widely differing methodologies in the pursuit of greater understanding of factors influencing youth outcomes in mentoring programs.

MENTORING OBSERVATIONS

Marcus, the author's Little Brother, is 9 years old and recently started the 3rd grade.[1] He is from a low-income, single-parent family headed by his mother. He has two older siblings, a 11-year-old sister and 14-year-old brother.

Overall, it is my impression that my relationship with Marcus has had a positive impact on several areas of his adjustment. In accordance with BB/BS program guidelines, a consistent pattern of weekly contact has been maintained for more than a year. Marcus and I, furthermore, have a relationship that is marked by easily observed feelings of mutual closeness and affection. Our relationship thus is characterized by several features similar to those indicated to be important for positive youth outcomes in mentoring programs (DuBois et al., in press; Rhodes, in press). Yet, consistent with findings of our meta-analysis, the extent of the gains that I have observed, which might be attributed to our relationship, have been modest and incremental rather than marked or large.

The most notable progress has been evident in areas in which I have specifically focused my efforts. These include, most notably, efforts to enhance Marcus' self-esteem and other aspects of his emotional well-being. Having observed him to make self-disparaging comments on several occasions early in our relationship, I made it a point to on a consistent basis provide specific, positive statements about his abilities and behavior toward others as these were evidenced in our interactions together. In numerous instances, he has later repeated these statements nearly verbatim, such as when he related to me, "I'm good at figuring out how stuff works," following observations that I had shared with him regarding his mechanical aptitude. It thus appears that validation of strengths within the mentoring relationship has helped Marcus to begin to internalize positive views of himself as part of his own self-concept (Harter, 1999). To further facilitate growth in Marcus' self-esteem, I have encouraged him to set meaningful goals in various areas of his life (e.g., school, sports) and to then strive to reach these. The value of this process is evident in Marcus now spontaneously engaging in such behavior himself. Illustratively, he recently announced that he had made a "challenge" to himself to learn all 50 state capitals even though his school assignment required him to learn only a portion of them. With further relevance to emotional well-being, the mentoring relationship appears to have helped alleviate noteworthy feelings of sadness and dysphoria that Marcus began to display after his brother and sister, with whom he enjoys very close relationships, were removed from the home by child and family services. Marcus' mother shared with me her impression that the additional time I spent with him following this event had a significant positive impact on Marcus' mood and overall outlook.

Efforts also have been made in the mentoring relationship to facilitate Marcus' academic adjustment, such as informal tutoring and help with homework. These have not been intensive or consistent facets of the relationship, however, and few, if any, gains are apparent that might be attributed to the activities involved. For the majority of the relationship, other outside services also have been lacking that might have helped to address Marcus' needs for support in this area. As a result, despite having previously been held back a grade, the possibility of doing so again was considered at the end of Marcus' second grade year. At this time, concerns noted included lack of progress in nearly all subject areas and frequent absences throughout the school year.

My experiences working with Marcus underscore the reality that attempting to ensure the positive development and adjustment of any youth can be an enormously challenging task. Inherent limits in the amount of time that mentors are able to devote to relationships, coupled with pre-existing problems and difficulties for many of the youth involved in programs, suggests that even modest inroads in selected areas or domains are likely to be hard-won accomplishments. Although not addressed to date in much research, my experiences suggest the possibility that there may be relatively greater potential for successful promotion and prevention efforts in mentoring relationships as compared to remediation of existing problems (Rhodes, in press). Thus, I have been able to observe success in efforts to enhance self-esteem and curb initial signs of possible depression with Marcus. By contrast, it has not proven possible to make significant inroads with respect to remediation of his more long-standing and extensive academic difficulties.

With regard to the program best practices referred to earlier (see Table 1), it is noteworthy that several of these factors have facilitated my ability to develop a strong and effective mentoring relationship with Marcus. One of these is the emphasis that is placed on careful matching of mentors and youth on relevant characteristics within BB/BS programs (Tierney, Grossman, & Resch, 1995). Marcus and I are both White and, of course, also both male. Yet, a more significant consideration for us has had to do with the less readily apparent concern of my significant limitations in physical activity and mobility (due to a chronic medical condition). Marcus was astutely assessed to be an appropriate match for me in this regard owing to his relatively young age and his own delays in motor development. Both of these considerations suggested to program staff that his needs for physical activity would be compatible with what I could provide. Even allowing for this, there have been occasions when Marcus has become frustrated and seemingly embarrassed by my physical limitations. With a less appropriately matched youth (e.g., an older teenager highly enthused about sports participation), it is not difficult to imagine how such reactions could be enough to derail the type of initial bonding that occurred for Marcus and I as we were able to engage in shared activities of mutual interest. These considerations imply that to yield optimal results mentor/youth matching needs to extend beyond efforts focused on relatively straightforward dimensions such as gender or race. It needs also to incorporate efforts to ensure compatibility with regard to attributes of mentors and youth that are less readily apparent, but still potentially quite influential for the development of their relationship.

One of the empirically-identified best practices was recruiting mentors with backgrounds in helping roles or professions. Although not recruited specifically for this reason, my background as a mental health professional nonetheless has proven advantageous in my relationship with Marcus. It has allowed me, for example, to both understand and respond effectively to various emotional and behavioral concerns exhibited by Marcus. These include his notable tendencies toward impulsivity and hyperactivity that have resulted in his receiving a probably accurate diagnosis of Attention Deficit Hyperactivity Disorder. If the behaviors involved were viewed as stemming from simply a "lack of discipline" or voluntary self-control, an adult interacting with a youth such as Marcus could easily "personalize" his or her struggles in this area, thus making it difficult for a positive bond to develop in the relationship. The same applies to my recognition of Marcus' tendencies toward strong attachments with adult caretaking figures and their likely basis in experiences of loss earlier in his development. In the beginning stages of our relationship, this understanding enabled me to not feel unduly "dismissed" when Marcus chose to end some of our outings after only a relatively short amount of time because of a desire to go home to see his mother. As our relationship has progressed, this appreciation also has allowed me to not feel overwhelmed or uncomfortable in response to indications of Marcus' close attachment to me, one of which his tendency during times of insecurity to want to refer to me as his "Dad."

These considerations notwithstanding, I also have benefitted from supervision from agency staff, another identified best practice. Illustratively, the BB/BS staff member fulfilling this role suggested at one point early on in my mentoring experience that I have Marcus over to my home as a way of helping to cultivate greater intimacy and comfort in our still evolving relationship. Breaking the somewhat monotonous routine we had gotten into of trips to the mall for a "games and popcorn," a night at my home did indeed prove a catalyst for Marcus and I to become closer and more relaxed in our interactions. I personally have not experienced a significant need for other, related best practices such as initial "pre-match" training or ongoing training once relationships are formed. It is noteworthy in this regard, however, that relationships of both Marcus' brother and sister with mentors assigned by the same BB/BS program each dissolved after only a relatively short period of time (prior to these children's removal from the home). Some of the factors contributing to these premature endings might have been avoided with provision of greater training for mentors, a program feature which is not presently required for BB/BS affiliates. Illustratively, the mentor for Marcus' sister reportedly picked her up for one of their first outings without first "checking in" with Marcus' mother to let her know where they would be going. This incident appeared to detract considerably from parental support for the relationship, a factor that our findings indicate can facilitate more positive outcomes in programs (see Table 1). An older, retired couple were assigned as mentors to Marcus' brother.

They expressed interest on several occasions in comparing notes with me and seeking my advice on challenging issues which arose in their efforts to work with this youth. These issues, unfortunately, were what ultimately led them to end the relationship after only a few months. Participation in a mutual support group for mentors, another best practice in our meta-analysis, seemingly might have proven particularly helpful for these mentors.

Returning to the relationship between Marcus and myself, a further program "best practice" deserving of note is agency-sponsored structured activities. Each month, the BB/BS affiliate sends out a schedule detailing several age-appropriate recreational and educational activities that they have organized or arranged for mentors and youth to participate in together. Marcus and I took particular advantage of these in the earliest stages of our relationship—examples include a roller skating party, Halloween celebration, and football clinic conducted by players from the local university team. These removed the burden of coming up with new things to do on a week-to-week basis and provided a comfortable group setting within which Marcus and I could gradually become at ease with one another. The significance of these benefits is underscored by the importance of regular contact as a necessary condition for mentoring effectiveness and by the need for feelings of security and closeness in relationships to have the opportunity to develop over time (Rhodes, in press).

CONCLUSION: A PROPOSED GENERAL FRAMEWORK FOR ENHANCING MENTORING PROGRAM EFFECTIVENESS

Overall, my experiences as a Big Brother to Marcus bear a close relation to empirically-observed trends in the effectiveness of mentoring programs for youth. They indicate, furthermore, that a participatory research approach can be of significant benefit for deepening and expanding our appreciation of factors influencing processes and outcomes in mentoring relationships. Considered together, the information and experiences available to me as a researcher and as a mentor are consistent in pointing toward the need for an approach to mentoring program development that is both intensive and broad-based. The key components of this approach are incorporated into the proposed framework for enhancing mentoring program effectiveness. The framework is comprised of two primary dimensions: (1) internally-focused or "inside" efforts to strengthen mentoring relationships as a core feature of programs and (2) externally-focused or "outside" efforts directed toward establishing effective linkages to other resources and services needed to promote positive outcomes for youth receiving mentoring.

From an "inside" perspective, it seems clear that programs should devote considerable resources to the implementation of best practices such as those discussed in this paper. These types of efforts should include both (a) program-wide innovations (e.g., regularly-occurring activities for mentors and youth), and (b) those geared toward ensuring the successful development of individual relationships (e.g, supervision from agency staff). Although less well-established, effectiveness also may be enhanced from an "outside" perspective when there is an effort by mentoring programs to integrate and connect their efforts with other services and resources important for positive youth development. Paralleling "inside" efforts at program development, it may be beneficial to direct such initiatives toward both (a) establishing linkages with outside resources and services at the program level (e.g., cooperative agreements or jointly sponsored activities with other agencies) and (b) development of coordinated or comprehensive service plans designed to address the differing needs of individual youth. These are not new concepts or ideas in the intervention literature (Bartholomew, Parcel, Kok, & Gottlieb, 2001). Yet, it is nevertheless the case that many, if not most, mentoring programs seem to currently operate for the most part as "stand alone" operations, with relatively few resources devoted to coordination with external agencies or services.

The major elements and assumptions of the proposed framework echo my experiences as a mentor. I would not have realized the success I have had so far in the absence of the kinds of strong internal support that relationships between mentors and youth receive within agencies such as BB/BS that are, in essence, specialists in the area of mentoring. Moreover, as illustrated by the dissolution of the mentoring relationships of Marcus' siblings, there is ample room for even those programs practicing a majority of identified best practices to further innovate and expand to better ensure successful relationship development. It is equally apparent that the efforts of a single mentor are not adequate to fully address the needs of youth such as Marcus. Illustrating the potential value and range of such linkages to outside resources, Marcus recently has been enrolled in and begun to benefit from academic tutoring services in an afterschool program, whereas his mother is now employed for the first time in several years with the help of a job training program. If pursued in an effective manner, a coordinated network of services with a strong mentoring relationship and program at its core could be a viable strategic framework for more fully realizing the substantial benefits that often are claimed for mentoring, but to date only rarely observed. The full range of available quantitative and qualitative methodologies should be utilized to maximum advantage in pursuing the development of this and other proposed frameworks for enhancing mentoring program effectiveness. By doing so, there will be greater opportunity for mentoring to be a useful tool in preparing youth and our society for success in the 21st century.

NOTE

1. Marcus is a fictitious name. Permission was obtained from both the youth and his mother to share the information that is included in this paper.

REFERENCES

America's Promise: The Alliance for Youth. (1999). *Report to the nation: 1999*. Alexandria, VA: Author.

Banyard, V. L., & Miller, K. E. (1998). The powerful potential of qualitative research for community psychology. *American Journal of Community Psychology, 26*, 485-505.

Bartholomew, L. K., Parcel, G. S., Kok, G., & Gottlieb, N. H. (2001). *Intervention mapping: Designing theory- and evidence-based health promotion programs*. Mountain View, CA: Mayfield Publishing Company.

Brydon-Miller, M., & Tolman, D. L. (2001). Making room for subjectivities: Remedies for the discipline of psychology. In D. L. Tolman & M. Brydon-Miller (Eds.), *From subjects to subjectivities: A handbook of interpretive and participatory methods* (pp. 319-327). New York: New York University Press.

Cooper, H. (1998). *Synthesizing research: A guide for literature reviews* (3rd ed.). Thousand Oaks, CA: Sage.

DuBois, D. L., Holloway, B. E., Valentine, J. C., & Cooper, H. (in press). Effectiveness of mentoring programs for youth: A meta-analytic review. *American Journal of Community Psychology*.

Freedman, M. (1992). *The kindness of strangers: Reflections on the mentoring movement*. Philadelphia: Public/Private Ventures.

Grossman, J. B., & Rhodes, J. E. (in press). The test of time: Predictors and effects of duration in youth mentoring relationships. *American Journal of Community Psychology*.

Harter, S. (1999). *The construction of the self: A developmental perspective*. New York: Guilford Press.

National Mentoring Working Group. (1991). *Mentoring: Elements of effective practice*. Washington, DC: National Mentoring Partnership.

Rhodes, J. E. (1994). Older and wiser: Mentoring relationships in childhood and adolescence. *Journal of Primary Prevention, 14*, 187-196.

Rhodes, J. E. (in press). *Stand by me: Risks and rewards in youth mentoring.* Cambridge, MA: Harvard University Press.

Tierney, J. P., Grossman, J. B., & Resch, N. L. (1995). *Making a difference. An impact study of Big Brothers/Big Sisters.* Public/Private Ventures, Philadelphia, PA.

Evaluation of an Incentive System at a Summer Camp for Youth Experiencing Homelessness

Laura A. Nabors
Annie Hines
Laura Monnier

University of Cincinnati

SUMMARY. Children who are homeless often experience emotional and behavioral problems. They also may have difficulty interacting with peers. Programs designed to reward positive behaviors may be successful in improving behavioral functioning for children experiencing emotional distress due to homelessness and related risk factors. Families experiencing homelessness may have a difficult time accessing mental health services. School settings may be optimal environments for implementing programs to improve behavioral and social development for these children. In this paper, we describe the implementation and outcomes of an incentive system, developed to improve school behaviors and interactions for children experiencing homelessness. This system was imple-

---

Address correspondence to: Laura Nabors, Department of Psychology, Room 429 Dyer Hall, Mail Location 376, University of Cincinnati, Cincinnati, OH 45221-376 (E-mail: naborsla@email.uc.edu).

The authors' appreciation is extended to the University of Cincinnati, Department of Psychology for funding this project and to Dr. Shear and Dr. Corcoran for mentoring and support. The authors also would like to thank staff at the Project Connect Office for their support of this project.

[Haworth co-indexing entry note]: "Evaluation of an Incentive System at a Summer Camp for Youth Experiencing Homelessness." Nabors, Laura A., Annie Hines, and Laura Monnier. Co-published simultaneously in *Journal of Prevention & Intervention in the Community* (The Haworth Press, Inc.) Vol. 24, No. 2, 2002, pp. 17-31; and: *Community Interventions to Create Change in Children* (ed: Lorna H. London) The Haworth Press, Inc., 2002, pp. 17-31. Single or multiple copies of this article are available for a fee from The Haworth Document Delivery Service [1-800-HAWORTH, 9:00 a.m. - 5:00 p.m. (EST). E-mail address: getinfo@haworthpressinc.com].

© 2002 by The Haworth Press, Inc. All rights reserved.

mented during a summer camp designed to enrich reading skills. Teachers and aides administered bracelets as secondary reinforcers for positive and prosocial behaviors. Children could purchase primary reinforcers, such as toys and art supplies, with the bracelets. Results were positive, supporting project activities. Future programs and evaluation projects should focus on delivering and evaluating prevention and therapy services for youth experiencing homelessness. *[Article copies available for a fee from The Haworth Document Delivery Service: 1-800-HAWORTH. E-mail address: <getinfo@haworthpressinc.com> Website: <http://www.HaworthPress.com> © 2002 by The Haworth Press, Inc. All rights reserved.]*

KEYWORDS. Homeless youth, prevention, behavioral modification

Due to public law 104-193 and changes to the welfare system, which have limited support for low-income families, more children and families have experienced homelessness in recent years. An increasing number of children experiencing homelessness are in elementary school and are from minority groups. These children often face behavioral and emotional problems, experience significant life stress, are absent from school, and typically are behind academically (Polakow, 1998; Alperstein, Rappaport, & Flanigan, 1988; Lindsey, 1998; Zima, Wells, & Freeman, 1994; Zima et al., 1999). They also have limited access to mental health services (Shirley, 1995). Participating in prevention programs in school may promote coping for these children (Nabors, Proescher, & DeSilva, 2001; Tashman et al., 2000).

The "Bracelet Behavior Program" at the Project Connect (PC) Summer Camp was an incentive system designed to promote positive behaviors and social skills for a group of children who were homeless. Because children experiencing homelessness are at increased risk for school problems and academic underachievement, behavior management plans, such as incentive systems, may be especially beneficial for this group (Polakow, 1998; Zima et al., 1994, 1999). Although there are many books and review articles discussing behavior management in the classroom, relatively few empirical studies are documented in the literature (Bergin & Bergin, 1999). Understanding the impact of programs designed to foster positive behaviors and social responsibility in school settings will enhance knowledge in the field.

In this paper, we present the results of an evaluation project in which quantitative and qualitative methods were used to examine the impact of the incentive system at the PC Summer Camp. Data were recorded in several ways. First, teachers and parents recorded their perceptions of the children's behavioral, emotional, and academic functioning at the start and end of the camp. Second, teaching assistants recorded children's positive and negative behaviors using event coding. Several evaluation questions were addressed. For example, gender differences were examined as well as classroom and age level differences. Also, regression analyses were used to examine predictors of bracelet totals and positive and negative behaviors. Information from this project was shared with camp administrators, in order to provide accountability data for program funders and to generate ideas for behavior management programming for future camps.

METHOD

Participants

A total of 99 children, whose families were experiencing homelessness, enrolled in the summer camp and 72 of these youth attended camp for two or more weeks. Parental consent was obtained to enroll 51 of these children, 23 boys and 28 girls, in this project. The age range for the sample was from 5 to 12 years, with a mean age of 8 years, 3 months. Forty-eight of the children were African-American and 3 were Caucasian. Camp attendance was variable, with children attending from 5 to 35 days, with a mean attendance of 22 days. Children whose parents rated their behaviors at home, $r = .50, p \leq .001$, and at school, $r = .37, p \leq .05$, as more positive had higher attendance.

Three experienced teachers, who were employed by the city schools, were hired to lead the three classes at the camp. The research assistant was a 22-year-old Caucasian female who was a senior at a local university. She also served as a teaching assistant for a class and was a paid employee/volunteer from the Americorp Services. The other teaching assistants also were college students participating in the Americorp Services. They received a weekly stipend and tuition remission for their work. There were six females, including the research assistant, and one male. Teaching assistants ranged in age from 18 to 22 years ($M = 20$). One female teaching assistant was African-American, the rest were Caucasian. Three females and one male recorded data in the behavior logs for this project.

Program Description. The summer camp was a summer school program emphasizing reading skills. Children worked on reading skills each morning. Academic activities focussed on learning vocabulary words, improving reading comprehension and spelling skills, and improving expressive writing and composition skills. Children participated in recreational activities in the afternoons. Weekly field trips designed to be either recreational (e.g., amusement park) or educational (e.g., children's museum) were an important camp activity.

Several enrichment activities were offered during the camp. For example, children participated in a weekly art class and weekly mental health prevention activities. One of the goals of the art class was to foster teamwork among the children. The mental health prevention activities addressed several goals related to conflict resolution, anger management, social skills, and group cohesion (Chapman-Weston & Weston, 1996; Nabors, 2001; Roehlkepartain & Leffert, 2000).

Measures

How My Child Is Doing Survey (Nabors et al., 2001). This measure examined parent perceptions of their child's behavioral, emotional, and academic functioning. There were five questions for rating the child's "acting out" behavior, social skills, grades, behavior at home, and sadness on four-point Likert scales. When making ratings, parents were instructed to rate their child's behavior (from poor to very good; very sad to happy) in comparison to other children in the same age range.

Teacher Survey of Student Progress (Nabors et al., 2001). This survey assessed teacher ratings of children's behavioral, emotional, and academic functioning for the same questions used on the parent measure. Researchers working at the Center for School Mental Health Assistance (CSMHA), at the University of Maryland, have received funding from the Agency for Healthcare Research and Quality to conduct studies to establish psychometric properties for this survey and the parent survey.

Procedure

Forty-six parents completed the *How My Child Is Doing Survey* (Nabors et al., 2001) when their child entered the program. Twenty-six parents completed the survey again, after 7 weeks, at the end of the program. Teachers completed the *Teacher Survey of Student Progress* (Nabors et al., 2001) for 45 of the children during the first and last week of camp. Teachers received a $30 gift certificate for completing multiple measures at the end of the camp.

Teachers and teaching assistants attended an orientation session the week before camp began. During this orientation, they received training on how to implement the Bracelet Program. The main goal for this program was to "encourage positive behavior." Teachers and teaching assistants awarded bracelets if the child was (1) being a role model for other children, (2) using anger management skills, (3) following directions, (4) sharing, (5) having good hygiene (brushing teeth and washing hands), and (6) exhibiting kind and/or helpful behavior.

Children earned both daily and weekly rewards based on the number of bracelets they had earned. At the end of the day, teachers recorded the number of bracelets each child had received in the child's bracelet log. Then, the child went to the prize room and handed in his or her bracelets to the research assistant. If a child earned 8 or more bracelets in a day, he or she was eligible for a daily prize. If a child earned at least eight bracelets in a day, he or she would receive a small prize, like a piece of candy or small toy (value about fifty cents), at the end of the day. If the child earned 10 or more bracelets per day, then the child was able to select a prize of greater value (about $1-$2), such as a pinwheel or ball.

Weekly rewards were based on the total number of bracelets earned per week. Teachers handed in bracelet logs, for all of the children in the class, to the research assistant each Friday. The research assistant calculated the total number of bracelets earned by each of the children. After doing this, she went to the classes and got small groups of children who went with her to the prize room and selected their "good behavior" rewards. Children could select a more expensive prize (from about $7-$12), such as a small, hand-held computer game or a Barbie doll, if they reached Level III by earning 45 to 50 bracelets in a week. At Level II, children had earned between 35 to 44 bracelets, and they could select a prize (valued at about $3 to $6), such as a package of markers and a coloring book or crossword puzzle books. At Level I, children had earned between 20 to 34 bracelets over the week, and they could select a prize of lesser value ($1 to $3), such as a deck of cards or a small stuffed animal or toy car.

Recording Events in Behavior Logs. Teaching assistants coded positive and negative behaviors in their logs (notebooks). They were instructed to record salient events representing "your perceptions of positive or negative behaviors exhibited by the children." Teaching assistants were not provided with operational definitions other than those provided for the Bracelet Program. However, they were instructed to provide antecedents and consequences for both positive and negative behavioral events as well as to record the initials, age, gender, and ethnicity of the child beside each event. They were asked to be as specific as possible and include all details related to the event (Bakeman & Gottman, 1986). The first author reviewed the logs on a weekly basis and provided written suggestions for improving the detail in notes about events, in terms of specifically recording the antecedents, behaviors, and consequences for each event. After the last week of camp, teaching assistants turned in logs and received a $40.00 gift certificate as an incentive for their work on this project.

After camp ended, the first and second authors independently reviewed the logs and independently developed behavioral categories for quantifying data in the logs. The raters then developed operational definitions for these categories based on consensus (agreement for each definition). Definitions of positive and negative behavior categories are presented in Table 1.

Four positive and four negative behavior categories were identified. The positive categories were (1) helping others, (2) following directions, (3) completing class work/on-task behaviors, and (4) exhibiting appropriate behaviors. The final category was subdivided into four sections: (a) positive behaviors, (b) behavior characteristic of being a "role model," (c) shar-

TABLE 1. Operational Definitions for Positive and Negative Behavior Categories

Behavior Category	Operational Definition
Helping Others	Showing kindness toward and assisting other children or adults (e.g., holding doors, helping others with work).
Following Directions	Following class rules. Listening to and following instructions given by adults (teachers and assistants; e.g., walking, not running, remaining quiet on the bus).
Completing Work/On-Task	Completing class work and assignments appropriately and enthusiastically. Child remains seated and is accomplishing assigned work.
Role Model	Child exhibits behavior that is exemplary and is a model for appropriate behavior for other children to follow.
Sharing/Taking Turns	Sharing bracelets, materials, food or drink, or toys with another child.
Unkind Behavior	Behavior that is unkind toward others, but does not involve physical aggression (e.g., teasing, name-calling).
Not Following Directions	Not following class rules or instructions given by an adult.
Not Doing Work/Off-Task	Child refuses to do class work. Child unable to sit still or concentrate on assignment. Child is distracted and does not finish assignments.

ing, and (d) turn-taking. The negative categories included (1) unkind behavior that was not physically violent, (2) not following directions/ breaking rules, (3) not doing class work/off-task behavior, and (4) exhibiting inappropriate behaviors. Again, the fourth category was subdivided into four sections: (a) negative behaviors (e.g., tantrums, complaining), (b) destroying property, (c) stealing, and (d) physical aggression.

After the operational definitions were developed, raters reviewed the logs a second time, and coded the events as belonging to one of the four positive or negative behavior categories (Bakeman & Gottman, 1986). Raters also recorded "key examples of common events," representing common negative or positive behaviors exhibited by the children.

Data Analyses

A hierarchical regression analysis was used to assess predictors of the number of bracelets earned by the children. A total score was derived for each child by dividing the total number of bracelets earned during the first seven weeks of camp by the number of days the child attended camp during this period. The final week of camp consisted of several field trips, a talent show for parents, and other activities to celebrate the end of camp. This week was not representative of a typical week, and therefore bracelets earned during this week were not included in final analyses. Additional regression analyses were used to examine predictors of the total number of positive and negative behaviors recorded in the logs.

Repeated measures analyses were used to examine differences in children's functioning from the start to the end of camp. Dependent variables were parent and teacher ratings of children's externalizing behavior at home and in the classroom, social skills, grades, and degree of sadness. Gender, age level (older versus younger children), and classroom setting (children were assigned to one of three classrooms) were independent variables, with number of bracelets earned and number of negative behaviors as covariates. One-way ANOVAs were used to assess for gender and age level differences in parent and teaching ratings at the start or end of camp. Correlational analyses to examine the relationships among variables, such as having a sibling in class and social skills, also were conducted.

RESULTS

Parent Perceptions of Children's Functioning. An ANOVA for parent ratings on the *How My Child Is Doing Survey* (Nabors et al., 2001) indicated that they perceived boys ($M = 3.09$, $SD = .54$) as exhibiting poorer behavior than girls ($M = 3.53$, $SD = .52$; $F(1, 24) = 4.49$, $p \leq .05$) at the end of camp. Other ANOVAs did not yield significant results. Repeated measures analyses indicated that parents did not perceive significant improvements in their child's acting out behaviors at home or at school, social skills, academic skills, or sadness from the beginning to the end of camp.

Teacher Perceptions of Children's Functioning

A repeated measures analysis indicated that teachers perceived older children to show higher academic skills compared to younger children, both at the start and end of camp, Wilks' Lambda = .606, $F(1, 40) = 25.96$, $p \leq .001$. Means and standard deviations for teacher ratings of areas on the *Teacher Survey* are presented in Table 2.

The interaction of age level and gender had a significant effect on teacher ratings of children's social skills, Wilks' Lambda = .888, $F(1,38) = 4.79$, $p \leq .05$. At the beginning of camp, teachers rated girls as having higher social skills than boys, irrespective of age level. At the end of camp, teachers reported higher social skills for younger boys than younger girls. In contrast, they reported lower scores in the area of social skills for older boys compared to older girls (see Table 2). Inter-

TABLE 2. Means and Standard Deviations for Teacher Ratings of Social Skills and Academic Achievement

Area on Teacher Survey	Age Level							
	Pretest				Posttest			
	Younger Ages		Older Ages		Younger Ages		Older Ages	
	M	(SD)	M	(SD)	M	(SD)	M	(SD)
Social Skills								
Boys	3.0	(.76)	2.5	(.84)	3.0[a]	(.54)	1.9[ab]	(.62)
Girls	3.2	(.43)	3.0	(.76)	2.9	(.47)	3.2[b]	(.46)
Academic Achievement[c]	.68	(1.49)	2.59	(.96)	.59	(1.3)	1.1	(1.5)

Note. [abc] Denotes a significant difference at $p \leq .05$.

estingly, having a sibling in the classroom was positively related to higher teacher ratings of children's social skills at the end of camp, $r = .373, p \leq .01$. Teachers did not report significant improvements in children's externalizing behaviors, sadness, or behaviors at home over the course of the program.

Bracelet Program. There was a significant difference in the number of bracelets earned per day between boys and girls, $F(1, 49) = 4.05, p \leq .05$. Specifically boys ($M = 6.59, SD = 1.23$) earned fewer bracelets than girls ($M = 7.35, SD = 1.44$) over the course of the camp. Class placement and age level did not affect the number of bracelets received by the children.

A hierarchical regression analysis indicated that parent and teacher ratings of children's externalizing or acting out behavior were significant predictors of the total number of bracelets, $F(4, 39) = 4.61, p \leq .01$. Positive ratings made by parents, in terms of their child's behavior, significantly predicted bracelet totals, Beta = .378, $t = 2.82, p \leq .01$. Conversely, teachers' ratings were inversely related to bracelet totals, in that children rated as exhibiting more acting out behavior were more likely to have more bracelets, Beta = $-.286$, $t = -2.09, p \leq .05$. Gender, classroom setting, and age level were not significant predictors. This model predicted 32% of the variance in bracelet total.

Analyses of Information in Behavior Logs. A formula for percent agreement (number of agreements divided by the number of agreements plus disagreements multiplied by 100) was used to determine interrater reliabilities for the positive and negative behavior categories (Bakeman & Gottman, 1986). Percentages representing interrater reliability as well as the percentages of behaviors recorded in each category are presented in Table 3.

Interrater reliabilities were high, ranging from 83% to 100% ($M = 96\%$). Teaching assistants recorded more positive ($n = 147$) than negative ($n = 125$) behaviors in logs, providing some support for the positive impact of the Bracelet Program. A majority of the material recorded in the logs pertained to following directions or rules, followed by recording appropriate and inappropriate behaviors. Interestingly, 61% of the appropriate behaviors were in the role model area, while 17% were in the areas of sharing and taking turns. Twenty-two percent were in the general category. This category represented several types of appropriate behaviors, such as not fighting when provoked by others, not responding to teasing from peers, and following individual behavior plans (e.g., "BJ met his behavior goal of not fighting with others today").

TABLE 3. Percent Agreement Between Raters for and Percent of Behaviors Recorded in Positive and Negative Behavior Categories

Behavioral Categories/ Subcategories	Percent Agreement	Percentage of Time Behavior Was Recorded
Positive Categories	98%	54%
Helping Others	98%	11%
Following Directions	93%	43%
Completing Work/On-Task	97%	17%
Appropriate Behavior	99%	27%
Other	98%	2%
Negative Categories	99%	46%
Unkind Behavior	100%	10%
Not Following Directions	99%	38%
Not Doing Work/Off-Task	98%	15%
Inappropriate Behaviors	100%	37%

Assistants' records indicated that 50% of the inappropriate behaviors were in the subcategory of physical aggression, 10% involved taking things or stealing, and 1% involved destruction of property. Forty-nine percent of the behaviors were in the general subcategory. Examples included: throwing a tantrum, misbehaving on this bus, complaining, lying to others, cheating during games, or encouraging other children to get in a fight. At times, teaching assistants reported reasons for children's negative behaviors, such as being angry with peers or having a hard time at home before coming to camp. The following quote is an example:

> During the small reading group activity J. R. (8-year-old boy) was being very disruptive. I (teaching assistant) decided to take him to see Ms. M. (teacher) to ask what we should do. Ms. M. told J. R. that since he had been disruptive all morning he would not be able to go swimming in the afternoon, because he would need to make up his reading work. J. R. cried and rushed to the bathroom. After this, he stayed in with me for lunch and I talked to him about what was going on with him. He told me that N. P. (9-year-old girl in his class) and M. D. (8-year-old boy in his class) had been laughing at him (because he could not read well) and he did not like it. J. R. said he wanted to read the book, but that he was mad at his classmates, so he could not do this. J. R. then began to read his assign-

ment and finished it. I decided to let him go swimming in the afternoon, because he had caught up on his reading.

This example was recorded toward the end of camp, and we noticed several other records that reported initial negative interactions that turned out positively during about the last two weeks of camp. This varied from events recorded at the beginning of the logs where negative behaviors often escalated into additional negative behaviors. This successful change did not appear to be noticed by teaching assistants, who consistently kept recording interactions that began negatively and ended positively as negative behaviors.

Positive Behaviors. Teaching assistants had recorded positive behavioral events for 37 of the 51 children in our sample. Number of positive behaviors recorded per child ranged from 1 to 11 ($M = 4$ to 5). Number of positive behaviors recorded in the logs was positively related to the total number of bracelets earned ($r = .323, p = .05$) and attendance ($r = .688, p \leq .001$), but was not significantly related to the total number of negative behaviors recorded in the logs. A hierarchical regression analysis indicated that parent ratings of children's behavior at home was a significant predictor (Beta = .45, $t = 2.65, p \leq .05$) of the total number of positive behaviors, accounting for 23% of the variance. Gender, age, classroom, and parent ratings of the child's behavior at school were also included in the model, but did not significantly predict positive behaviors.

Negative Behaviors. Teaching assistants recorded negative behavioral events for 37 of the children (this group of students included different children than the records of positive behavioral events). Results from an ANOVA indicated that there was a significant gender difference in the total number of negative behaviors exhibited by boys and girls, $F(1, 49) = 6.13, p \leq .05$. Teaching assistants recorded more negative behaviors for boys ($M = 5.52, SD = 3.44$) than for girls ($M = 3.14, SD = 3.40$). The range for negative behaviors for boys was zero to thirteen and for girls it was zero to twelve. No age level differences or differences among classrooms were found. Regression analyses did not reveal significant predictors for the total number of negative behaviors.

DISCUSSION

Results revealed that boys might benefit from additional prevention efforts to improve their classroom functioning and social skills. Two sources of information, parent ratings and data recorded by teaching assistants, indicated that boys were more at risk for exhibiting negative or acting out behaviors compared to girls. Successful behavior was often defined as being a role model, helping others, or following rules and instructions. Consequently, behavior management planning for boys, especially those who are identified as exhibiting acting out or aggressive behaviors, should focus on increasing positive behaviors, such as setting an example for peers by following class rules.

Parent reports revealed that they viewed girls as exhibiting higher social skills than boys at the end of the camp. Conversely, teacher perceptions of the children's social skills were affected by age and gender. Also, teacher ratings of social skills at the end of camp indicated that if a sibling was in the room, children exhibited higher levels of social skills. Perhaps the sibling served as a role model or coach; qualitative research may be helpful in investigating this idea. Because many factors may have impacted children's social interactions, it may be advisable to develop individualized plans to improve social skills for at-risk children. Further, it will be important to use observational methods to gain a more comprehensive picture of social interactions in future studies.

Parent ratings of their child's acting out behaviors (e.g., low level of acting out) were positively associated with the bracelets their children earned and positive behaviors recorded in the logs. Thus, parent reports of children's behavioral functioning was a good indicator of their level of success at camp. Having parents complete a survey, such as the *How My Child Is Doing Survey* (Nabors et al., 2001), prior to camp might provide important information about children who are likely to be well behaved. Our results suggested that parent reports were not related to documentation of negative behaviors. In-person interviews may be helpful in gaining information about youth who may exhibit behavior problems. Learning about children who might have problems in the classroom or with their behavior before camp begins would allow teachers to develop appropriate prevention plans.

Anecdotal information from teaching assistants, and an in-depth review of chains of events recorded in the logs by the first and second authors, indicated that toward the end of camp children were better able to turn around a negative sequence of behavior and act more positively. At times, the teaching assistants were not aware of this gradual change. We recommended that paraprofessionals working with the children next year be reminded of the importance of rewarding or reinforcing children for small, positive changes in their reactions to instruction or discipline. Furthermore, records in the logs indicated that once a child began to exhibit good behaviors, these responses tended to generalize (i.e., records of good behaviors in the logs often increased; Skinner, 1953). Unfortunately, the opposite was also true, and when children began to behave negatively it could take some time for their behaviors to improve.

Staff might benefit from further instruction about rewarding positive behaviors and reducing negative behaviors. Although the book is written for parents, Lynn Clark (1985) provides a detailed and thorough explanation of behavior management plans for children, in *SOS! Help for Parents*. The principles described in this book are applicable to the classroom, and teachers could explain the guidelines to parents so that behavioral goals at school and at home are consistent and promote generalization of positive behaviors. Bergin and Bergin (1999) also provide useful ideas for promoting self-control and positive behaviors in the classroom. In addition, *The Handbook of School-Based Interventions* (Cohen & Fish, 1993) is a good resource for developing prevention programs to address discipline problems, impulsivity, as well as disruptive, aggressive, and destructive behaviors in classroom settings.

Shortcomings. Several shortcomings existed for this study. For example, it is not possible to isolate the impact of all the different interventions (e.g., incentive system, mental health prevention activities, art class, reading activities) that occurred over the course of the camp. The Bracelet Program was one intervention among many (e.g., mental health prevention classes, art classes), and therefore other interventions may have influenced children's behaviors (Mercier, Fournier, & Peladeau, 1992).

Moreover, the generalizability of our results is limited because there was not a comparison group. Additionally, our models predicted only a modest amount of the variation in positive behaviors and bracelets earned by youth, but we were not successful in understanding the factors related to negative behaviors. We may have been able to gain a better understanding of the children's behaviors if we had used measures and observational systems with established validity. Our review of the logs indicated that although they received weekly instruction, teaching assistants were not adept at recording antecedents and consequences for behaviors. Thus, further qualitative research, using ethnographic techniques to "take a deeper look" at the causes and consequences of behaviors, is recommended. Anecdotal reports from teaching assistants suggested that children, especially boys, with more significant behavior problems tended to leave camp. It may be that some of the children most in need of services were not receiving them.

It will be important to develop strategies to reach these children and retain them in the program.

In summary, results provided preliminary support for continuing the use of the Bracelet Program to promote positive behaviors at the PC Summer Camp. Results from our evaluation identified areas for improving prevention efforts in future years. School-based programs, like this one, may be ideal for providing prevention service to youth who have limited access to mental health services (Nabors et al., 2001; Tashman et al., 2000). It is our hope that policy makers, teachers, school administrators, parents, clinicians, and researchers will strive to implement prevention and therapy services for youth experiencing homelessness in schools. It will be important to examine the relationship between these activities and academic achievement in future studies.

REFERENCES

Bakeman, R., & Gottman, J. M. (1986). Observing interaction: An introduction to sequential analysis. New York, NY: Cambridge University Press.

Bergin, C., & Bergin, D. A. (1999). Classroom discipline that promotes self-control. *Journal of Applied Developmental Psychology, 20,* 189-206.

Chapman-Weston, D., & Weston, M. (1996). *Playwise: 365 fun-filled activities for building character, conscience, and emotional intelligence in children.* New York, NY: G. Putnam's Sons.

Clark, L. (1985). *SOS! Help for parents: A practical guide for handling common everyday behavior problems.* Bowling Green, KY: Parents Press.

Cohen, J. J., & Fish, M. C. (1993). *Handbook of school-based interventions: Resolving student problems and promoting healthy educational environments.* San Francisco, CA: Jossey-Bass.

Lindsey, E. W. (1998). The impact of homelessness and shelter life on family relationships. *Family Relations: Interdisciplinary Journal of Applied Family Studies, 47,* 243-252.

Mercier, C., Fournier, L., & Peladeau, N. (1992). Program evaluation of services for the homeless: Challenges and strategies. *Evaluation and Program Planning, 15,* 417-426.

Nabors, L. A. (2000). *Empowerment zone project: Manual of mental health prevention and character education activities for teachers, counselors, and clinicians.* Baltimore, MD: Center for School Mental Health Assistance (CSMHA), Department of Psychiatry, University of Maryland.

Nabors, L. A., Proescher, E., & DeSilva, M. (2001). School-based mental health prevention activities for homeless and at-risk youth. *Child and Youth Care Forum, 30,* 3-18.

Polakow, V. (1998). Homeless children and their families: The discards of the postmodern 1990s. In S. Books (Ed.), *Invisible children in the society and its* schools. *Sociocultural, political, and historical studies in education* (pp. 3-22). Mahwah, NJ: Lawrence Erlbaum Associates.

Roehlkepartain, J. L., & Leffert, N. (2000). *What young children need to succeed: Working together to build assets from birth to age 11*. Minneapolis, MN: Free Spirit Publishing.

Shirley, A. (1995). Special needs of vulnerable and underserved populations: Models, existing and proposed, to meet them. *Pediatrics, 96*, 858-863.

Skinner, B. F. (1953). *Science and human behavior*. New York: Free Press.

Tashman, N. A., Weist, M. D., Acosta, O., Bickham, N. L., Grady, M., Nabors, L., & Waxman, R. (2000). Toward the integration of prevention research and expanded school mental health programs. *Children's Services: Social Policy, Research, and Practice, 3*, 97-115.

Zima, B. T., Bussing, R., Bystritsky, M., Widawski, M. H., Belin, T. R., & Benjamin, B. (1999). Psychosocial stressors among sheltered homeless children: Relationship to behavior problems and depressive symptoms. *American Journal of Orthopsychiatry, 69*, 127-133.

Zima, B. T., Wells, K., & Freeman, H. E. (1994). Emotional and behavioral problems and severe academic delays among sheltered homeless children in Los Angeles County. *American Journal of Public Health, 84*, 260-264.

Prevention of Victimization: *Survival Skills* for Urban Youth

Elena Mikalsen
John P. Vincent
Gerald E. Harris

University of Houston

SUMMARY. Children are frequently exposed to violence at school or in their neighborhood, resulting in multiple negative psychological effects, including anxiety, depression, low self-esteem, isolation, hopelessness, and Posttraumatic Stress Disorder. The present study evaluated the unique prevention program implemented in inner city parks designed to prevent the development of short- and long-term consequences of exposure to chronic violence. Results indicated that participants benefited significantly from the program, as evidenced by a decrease in endorsement of submissive conflict resolution strategies and behavioral problems. Higher self-esteem was related to increased program gains. Gender emerged as another moderator, while age was unrelated to improvement. *[Article copies available for a fee from The Haworth Document Delivery Service: 1-800-HAWORTH. E-mail address: <getinfo@haworthpressinc.com> Website: <http://www.HaworthPress.com> © 2002 by The Haworth Press, Inc. All rights reserved.]*

Address correspondence to: Elena Mikalsen, University of Houston, Department of Psychology, 126 Heyne, Houston, TX 77204-5022 (E-mail: elena_mikalsen@hotmail.com).

This project has been supported by a grant from the Hogg Foundation of Mental Health.

[Haworth co-indexing entry note]: "Prevention of Victimization: *Survival Skills* for Urban Youth." Mikalsen, Elena, John P. Vincent, and Gerald E. Harris. Co-published simultaneously in *Journal of Prevention & Intervention in the Community* (The Haworth Press, Inc.) Vol. 24, No. 2, 2002, pp. 33-44; and: *Community Interventions to Create Change in Children* (ed: Lorna H. London) The Haworth Press, Inc., 2002, pp. 33-44. Single or multiple copies of this article are available for a fee from The Haworth Document Delivery Service [1-800-HAWORTH, 9:00 a.m. - 5:00 p.m. (EST). E-mail address: getinfo@haworthpressinc.com].

KEYWORDS. Victim, prevention, community

Chronic victimization of children has become a significant problem in our society. Between 10 and 20% of children are chronically victimized at schools (Olweus, 1991; U.S. Department of Education & U.S. Department of Justice, 1999), and between 30 and 91% of children witness violence in their environments (Osofsky, 1995; Pynoos & Eth, 1985). In 1999, a one-month survey indicated that 11% of students had missed one or more days of school because of fear of violence (Center for Disease Control, 1999), and it has been estimated that, every day, 160,000 U.S. children miss school because of fear of being bullied (Seppa, 1996).

Consequences of exposure to chronic violence include anxiety, depression, low self-esteem, isolation from peers, hopelessness, and Posttraumatic Stress Disorder (Besag, 1989; Callaghan & Joseph, 1995; Hyman, Zelikoff, & Clarke, 1988; Osofsky, 1995; Pynoos & Eth, 1985). Victims often respond to bullying either with submissiveness or aggression, which could place them at greater risk for continuing victimization and greater stress (Egan & Perry, 1998; Pellegrini, Bartini, & Brooks, 1999; Sharp, 1996). A study by DuRant, Cadenhead, Pendergrast, Slavens, and Linder (1994) showed that previous victimization and exposure to violence were the strongest predictors of violence by teenagers.

Given the alarming prevalence rates and the negative consequences of victimization, implementation of prevention programs for children at risk is very important. Unfortunately, there is a dearth of victimization prevention programs. The few programs that do attempt to prevent the consequences of exposure to chronic violence are implemented with either the general population or with children at risk for becoming perpetrators. There is some evidence that victims of peer aggression can be helped successfully. One program (Cowen, Wyman, Work, & Iker, 1995), which targeted victims specifically, resulted in successfully reducing children's anxiety and increasing their feelings of being able to handle stressful situations.

In response to the need for services for victims, in 1996, the Victims' Resource Institute at the University of Houston implemented the *Survival Skills* program by exporting school-based techniques to an urban park setting. The program was implemented in high-crime parks with children at risk for exposure to chronic violence in their communities. The program was designed to apply the successful elements of other prevention efforts to children and adolescents who were identified as being at risk for victimization. By providing children with "survival skills" such as strategies for assertive conflict resolution, problem-solving, and anger management, the program aimed to prevent the development of short- and long-term consequences of being exposed to violence. In addition, the program aimed to extend prevention services to an important community setting. While community parks often play a central role in the lives of children and adolescents in high-crime neighborhoods, they also often suffer from lack of supervision and structure. Providing survival skills in such an environment holds the promise of equipping children with tools that will help reduce the likelihood they will fall victim to violence.

The present study evaluated the impact of this park-based prevention program on children's endorsement of aggressive, assertive, and submissive conflict resolution strategies, and on self- and parent-reported behavioral problems. In addition, several potential moderators of children's response to this prevention program were identified from the literature and evaluated in this study. Age was one of the moderators, since younger children have found prevention programs more helpful and informational and reported using the skills learned more frequently than older children (Finkelhor & Dziuba-Leatherman, 1995). The moderating effects of gender were examined as well. While some prevention programs have found that boys and girls responded differently (Esbensen & Osgood, 1999; Finkelhor & Dziuba-Leatherman, 1995), no consistent gender differences have emerged. Finally, the potential moderating effects of self-esteem were examined, since higher self-esteem has been linked both theoretically (Egan & Perry, 1998) and empirically (Baelle & Wertheim, 1992; Vicknair, 1996) to more positive outcomes from intervention programs.

METHOD

Participants

Children and adolescents regularly attending inner city Houston parks and playgrounds were recruited for participation. Fifty-five children (mean age–11.4, age range–5-15) participated in data collection. Participants were 61% males and 39% females and represented diverse ethnic backgrounds: 79% Hispanic, 16% Caucasian, and 5% African-American. Forty-nine participants provided information on exposure to violence. Of these participants, 60% reported knowing of gangs present in their neighborhoods, 25.5% had handled a gun, 5.5% reported being gang members, and 27.3% reported having experienced a traumatic event.

Program Description

Parks were selected on the basis of (a) the history of recent violence, (b) suspicion or reports of gang activity, and (c) child and parent reports of persistent bullying or other violence occurring at the park site. Parks were equipped with a quiet indoor facility, as well as an engaging outdoor recreation area (field, court, or playground). The program was implemented a total of ten times in eight different parks.

The program included six to ten hours of weekly sessions consisting of didactic presentations, group discussions, role-plays, and other activities. The program was group-based and each group consisted of five to eight children, a group leader, and a research assistant. Each session reserved 15-30 minutes of activity time for practice of newly learned skills. Appropriate skills and interactions were modeled and reinforced by staff during these activity times. The program consisted of the following components: Training in risk identification, problem-solving, anger management and emotional regulation, and conflict resolution.

Measures

Participants provided responses to a comprehensive assessment battery before and after their participation in the program.

Demographic Information Questionnaire. The Demographic Information Questionnaire is designed to obtain sociodemographic information about participants and their families.

Children's Action Tendencies Scale (CATS, Deluty, 1979). The CATS is a self-report measure of aggressive, assertive, and submissive conflict resolution styles in children and adolescents. Children are asked to respond as to which of the three styles they would endorse to manage 13 daily conflict situations, such as arguing with a peer. The scale has demonstrated adequate test-retest ($r = .44-.70$) and split-half ($r = .63-.77$) reliabilities, as well as evidence of its concurrent validity with parent- and peer-report (Deluty, 1979).

Child Behavior Checklist (CBCL, Achenbach, 1991). The CBCL provides a comprehensive assessment of child and adolescent psychosocial adjustment. The parent-report checklist consists of 20 items measuring social competence and 118 items describing behavior problems, each item rated in terms of the frequency of occurrence in the past six months. Scoring is based on age and gender norms and yields ten first-order factors and two broad-band second-order factors of internalizing and externalizing problems (Achenbach, 1991). The CBCL has been subjected to extensive validation and reliability studies (Achenbach, 1991).

The Youth Self-Report (YSR, Achenbach & Edelbrock, 1987). The Youth Self-Report measure is a self-report version of the CBCL designed for older (11 years old and above) children and adolescents. The YSR and CBCL share the same underlying empirically-based classification system of child and adolescent psychopathology. The validity and reliability of the YSR have been well-supported (Achenbach & Edelbrock, 1987). Self-report data supplemented assessment of difficulties that may not be apparent to parents.

Piers-Harris Self-Concept Scale (Piers, 1984). The Scale is an 80-item, self-report measure designed to assess child and adolescent self-esteem. Six cluster scores: Behavior, Intellectual & School Status; Physical Appearance & Attributes; Anxiety; Popularity; and Happiness & Satisfaction, as well as the total score are used to identify areas of relative strength and vulnerability in children. The Piers-Harris test-retest reliability coefficients have ranged from .42 (over 8 months) to .96 (over 3 to 4 weeks). Internal consistency estimates for the total score range from .88 to .93 (Piers, 1984).

Therapists

Survival Skills group leaders were trained graduate students in the clinical psychology doctoral program at the University of Houston. Co-facilitators of the program were postbaccalaureate and undergraduate research assistants. A manualized treatment protocol was followed, and group leaders were supervised by a Clinical Psychologist on a weekly basis in order to maintain treatment integrity and monitor program implementation.

RESULTS

Examination of the participants' scores indicated that this prevention sample did not appear to have any clinically important significant difficulties prior to their participation in the prevention program. On average, participants tended to endorse more assertive than submissive or aggressive conflict resolution strategies and report average self-esteem.

Main Analyses

Conflict Resolution Strategies. Repeated measures analyses of variance (ANOVAs) were utilized to examine the degree of pre-post changes in the participants' endorsement of aggressive, assertive, and submissive conflict resolution strategies. A significant difference was found in participants' pre-post endorsement of submissive conflict resolution strategies, $F(1, 45) = 4.15, p < .05$. As hypothesized, the participants endorsed fewer submissive conflict resolution strategies after their participation in the program. Table 1 presents the results. The hypotheses that participants would endorse fewer aggressive conflict resolution strategies and more assertive conflict resolution strategies after participation in the program were not confirmed.

Behavioral Symptoms. Repeated measures ANOVAs were utilized to examine the hypothesis predicting pre-post decreases in internalizing and externalizing symptoms. As can be seen in Table 1, a significant difference was found in parent-reported level of externalizing symptoms, $F(1, 6) = 7.41, p < .05$. Consistent with the hypothesis, the participants' parents reported significantly lower level of externalizing symptoms at the end of the program. No significant differences were found in pre-post parent-reported internalizing symptoms or in child-reported behavior problems.

TABLE 1. Means, Standard Deviations, and ANOVA Results for the Outcome Variables

	Pre		Post		
Variable	M	SD	M	SD	F
All Participants					
Aggressiveness	7.40	4.54	7.60	5.86	.40
Assertiveness	19.27	2.52	20.17	3.57	3.32
Submissiveness	12.10	3.91	11.23	3.86	4.15*
CBCL-Internalizing	57.00	7.57	54.75	6.97	2.20
CBCL-Externalizing	52.44	7.68	51.50	8.77	7.41*
YSR-Internalizing	51.34	10.09	49.39	14.22	1.22
YSR-Externalizing	51.91	12.96	52.13	15.62	.01

*$p < .05$

Self-Esteem

Participants' median score on self-esteem (54) was used to divide the sample into "low" (Piers-Harris score of 54 or below, n = 12) and "high" (Piers-Harris score above 54, n = 15) on self-esteem. The median score was close to the median score of the normative sample for the Piers-Harris (53.4). Two (self-esteem: high or low) × 2 (time: pre or post) repeated measures ANOVAs were conducted to analyze the impact of self-esteem on the pre-post changes in endorsement of each of the conflict resolution strategies.

Table 2 presents the means and standard deviations for assertiveness and aggressiveness by the self-esteem group. There was a significant impact of self-esteem, $F(1, 25) = 10.20$, $p < .01$ on the participants' endorsement of assertive conflict resolution strategies. Higher self-esteem was related to more frequent endorsement of assertive conflict resolution strategies. More importantly, participants classified as "high" in self-esteem decreased, while participants classified as "low" in self-esteem increased, in the endorsement of aggressive conflict resolution strategies, as indicated by a significant interaction between time and self-esteem, $F(1, 25) = 5.46$, $p < .05$. The results partially supported the hypothesis of higher pretreatment self-esteem related to greater pre-post improvement.

TABLE 2. Means for Aggressiveness and Assertiveness for Self-Esteem Groups

Variable	Pre		Post	
	M	SD	M	SD
Aggressiveness				
Self-esteem*				
Low	7.67	4.10	10.25	5.51
High	4.40	4.32	3.67	3.44
Assertiveness				
Self-esteem**				
Low	18.17	2.66	18.50	2.84
High	20.33	2.66	22.20	2.54

* Interaction between time and self-esteem at $p < .05$

** Self-esteem main effect at $p < .01$

Age

The impact of age on the pre-post change in the endorsement of conflict resolution strategies and level of behavioral symptoms was examined utilizing 2 (age: young or old) × 2 (time: pre or post) repeated measures ANOVAs. Participants' median age was used to divide the sample into "younger" (10 years old and below, n = 30) and "older" (10 years old and above, n = 25) groups. There was no support found for the hypothesis that pre-post changes in behavior and endorsement of conflict resolution strategies are due to age.

Gender

The hypothesis of the impact of gender on the pre-post change in the endorsement of conflict resolution strategies and level of behavioral symptoms was examined utilizing 2 (gender: male or female) × 2 (time: pre or post) repeated measures ANOVAs. Analyses of the entire sample revealed significant interactions between gender and time on child-reported internalizing symptoms, $F(1, 21) = 7.20, p < .05$ and endorsement of aggressive conflict resolution strategies, $F(1, 43) = 4.07, p < .05$. Table 3 presents the means and standard deviations for YSR-internalizing and aggressive responding for each gender. According to self-report, boys decreased while girls increased in their internalizing symptoms over the course of their participation. In addition, while boys increased, girls decreased in their endorsement of aggressive conflict resolution strategies through their participation in the program.

TABLE 3. Means for YSR-Internalizing and Aggressiveness for Females and Males

Variable	Pre		Post	
	M	SD	M	SD
YSR-Internalizing*				
Females	50.64	10.55	53.18	10.37
Males	52.17	10.06	45.92	16.70
Aggressiveness*				
Females	7.78	3.77	6.28	3.20
Males	7.17	5.08	8.21	6.76

* Interaction between time and gender at $p < .05$.

DISCUSSION

The major goals of the study were to evaluate the effectiveness of the *Survival Skills* prevention program and to explore whether participants' self-esteem, gender, and age were related to greater benefits gained from participation. This evaluation allowed exploration of the utility of implementing community prevention programs for children at risk for developing negative consequences of exposure to victimization.

Using a pre-post evaluation design, it was found that program participants did benefit from participation. Participants endorsed fewer submissive conflict resolution strategies and were reported by parents to exhibit significantly lower levels of externalizing symptoms at the end of the program. Responding to conflict situations submissively has been linked with greater risk for being victimized (Sharp, 1996), therefore, the program may have reduced participants' victimization risk. These positive findings are consistent with previous findings of the effectiveness of other prevention efforts for victims (Cowen et al., 1995; Finkelhor et al., 1995).

Important findings also emerged with regard to participants' preparticipation levels of self-esteem. Participants' level of self-esteem was positively related to their benefit from participation. This finding is consistent with findings in other research areas that self-esteem is related to positive treatment outcomes (Baelle & Wertheim, 1992; Vicknair, 1996). It is also consistent with theoretical suggestions (Cowen et al., 1995; Egan & Perry, 1998) that self-esteem contributes to resilience by enhancing coping with stressors in the environment. In this study, the participants with higher self-esteem endorsed fewer aggressive and more assertive conflict-resolution strategies at the end of the program. This pattern of responding may be important in preventing participants' engagement in dangerous conflict situations (Salmivalli, Karhunen, & Lagerspetz, 1996). Self-esteem emerged as a possible moderator to consider when implementing similar prevention programs. Future programs could address this finding by including intervention strategies specifically designed to empower children with lower self-esteem.

Interesting findings were obtained when gender effects were examined. According to self-report, boys experienced fewer internalizing symptoms after participation in the program and endorsed more aggressive conflict-resolution strategies, while girls experienced more internalizing symptoms and endorsed fewer aggressive conflict resolution strategies at the end of the program. Since participants in this prevention sample did not exhibit clinical levels of internalizing problems prior to participation in the program, it is difficult to determine whether the pre-post changes in behavioral symptoms were meaningful. However, the findings do point to the possible moderating effects of gender. A possible explanation for the differential findings with regard to gender is that the content of the program impacted boys and girls differently.

Interestingly, while it has been found that younger children obtained greater benefits from participation in other prevention programs (Finkelhor & Dziuba-Leatherman, 1995), this study did not obtain similar findings. It appears that the age of participants did not interact with the improvements, possibly indicating that *Survival Skills* effectively targeted participants of all ages. This study did not provide definitive answers with regard to the impact of age on program outcome. Future investigations might continue to examine this moderator in order to evaluate whether children's developmental level influences their gains from similar prevention programs.

The present exploratory study had several limitations. First, implementing a prevention program in a community setting presented multiple challenges, such as attrition, for example. Future prevention efforts should try to ensure cooperation from prevention sites, participants, and participants' parents in order to reduce attrition and improve data collection. Second, the lack of a control group restricted generalization of the findings, leading to the possibility that other factors may have accounted for the positive results, such as participants simply improving with time. Finally, no follow up data were collected to measure longer-term benefits of participation.

Despite the limitations, the results of this evaluation demonstrated that programs targeting potential victims of violence and focusing on prosocial skills training may be able to prevent some of the negative consequences of exposure to violence. The *Survival Skills* program was found effective in decreasing children's submissive responding, externalizing problems, and boys' internalizing problems. Externalizing problems, internalizing problems, and submissive responding to conflict have been linked with greater risk for victimization (Egan & Perry, 1998; Sharp, 1996). Interventions that effectively target these variables could, therefore, have a significant impact on reducing children's future vulnerability. The program was an important step to providing much needed prevention services for children who are at risk for experiencing negative consequences of exposure to violence. The program not only demonstrated positive results with regards to its effectiveness, but also identified an important moderating role of self-esteem in producing positive outcomes for participants.

REFERENCES

Achenbach, T. (1991). *Manual for the Child Behavior Checklist/4-18 and 1991 profile*. Burlington, VT: University of Vermont.

Achenbach, T., & Edelbrock, C. (1987). *Manual for the Youth Self-Report and profile*. Burlington, VT: University of Vermont.

Baelle, W. K., & Wertheim, E. H. (1992). Predictors of outcome in the treatment of bulimia nervosa. *British Journal of Clinical Psychology, 31*, 330-332.

Baker, K., Pollack, M., & Kohn, I. (1995). Violence prevention through informal socialization: An evaluation of the South Baltimore Youth Center. *Studies on Crime and Crime Prevention, 4*, 61-85.

Besag, V. E. (1989). *Bullies and victims in schools: A guide to understanding and management*. Philadelphia, PA: Open University Press.

Callaghan, S., & Joseph, S. (1995). Self-concept and peer victimization among schoolchildren. *Personality and Individual Differences, 18*, 161-163.

Center for Disease Control. (1999). *Morbidity and Mortality Weekly Report, 48*. Washington, DC: Author.

Cowen, E. L., Wyman, P. A., Work, W. C., & Iker, M. R. (1995). A preventive intervention for enhancing resilience among highly stressed urban children. *The Journal of Primary Prevention, 15*, 247-260.

Deluty, R. H. (1979). Children's Action Tendency Scale: A self-report measure of aggressiveness, assertiveness, and submissiveness in children. *Journal of Consulting and Clinical Psychology, 47*, 1061-1071.

DuRant, R. H., Cadenhead, C., Pendergrast, R. A., Slavens, G., & Linder, C. W. (1994). Factors associated with the use of violence among urban Black adolescents. *American Journal of Public Health, 84*, 612-617.

Egan, S. K., & Perry, D. G. (1998). Does low self-regard invite victimization? *Developmental Psychopathology, 34*, 299-309.

Esbensen, F., & Osgood, D. W. (1999). Gang Resistance Education and Training (GREAT): Results from the national evaluation. *Journal of Research in Crime and Delinquency, 36*(2), 194-225.

Finkelhor, D., & Dziuba-Leatherman, J. (1995). Victimization prevention programs: A national survey of children's exposure and reactions. *Child Abuse and Neglect, 19*, 129-139.

Hyman, I. A., Zelikoff, W., & Clarke, J. (1988). Psychological and physical abuse in the schools: A paradigm for understanding Post-Traumatic Stress Disorder in children and youth. *Journal of Traumatic Stress, 1*, 243-267.

Nolen-Hoeksema, S. (1992). Children coping with uncontrollable stressors. *Applied and Preventive Psychology, 1*, 183-189.

Olweus, D. (1991). Bully/victim problems among schoolchildren: Basic facts and effects of a school based intervention program. In D. J. Pepler & K.H. Rubin (Eds.), *The development and treatment of childhood aggression*. Hillsdale, NJ: Erlbaum.

Osofky, J. D. (1995). The effects of exposure to violence on young children. *American Psychologist, 50*, 782-788.

Pellegrini, A. D., Bartini, M., & Brooks, F. (1999). School bullies, victims, and aggressive victims. *Journal of Educational Psychology, 91*, 216-224.

Piers, E. V. (1984). *Piers-Harris Children's Self-Concept Scale*. Los Angeles, CA: Western Psychological Services.

Pynoos, R. S., & Eth, S. (1985). Children traumatized by witnessing acts of personal violence: Homicide, rape and suicide behavior. In S. Eth and R. S. Pynoos (Eds.), *Posttraumatic Stress Disorder in Children*. Washington, DC: American Psychiatric Press.

Salmivalli, C., Karhunen, J., & Lagerspetz, K. J. (1996). How do the victims respond to bullying? *Aggressive Behavior, 22*, 99-109.

Seppa, N. (1996). Keeping schoolyards safe from bullies. *Monitor: American Psychological Association, 27*, 41.

Sharp, S. (1996). Self-esteem, response style, and victimization. *School Psychology International, 17*, 347-357.

U.S. Department of Education, & U.S. Department of Justice, National Center for Education Statistics & Bureau of Justice Statistics. (1999). *Indicators of school crime and safety* (NCJ Publication No. 178906). Washington, DC: Authors.

Vicknair, J. A. (1996). *Self-esteem as a predictor of reactions of child and adolescent victims of violent crime*. Unpublished master's thesis, University of Houston, Houston, Texas.

Urban Children's Video Production and Performance-Based Programming: Implications for Learning and Cross-Cultural Friendships

Laura Knight Lynn

Prism Community Institute

Carol Harding
Bijai Rai
Stephen McManus
Kenzie Kitcharoen

Loyola University Chicago

Lisa Sweatt

California Polytechnic University

SUMMARY. This exploratory study investigated the impact of creative summer programming for urban children. Both qualitative and quantitative research methods were employed during a six-week summer program that offered video production and performance-based activities. An important feature of this study was the inclusion of children's own self-reports. Findings revealed an increase in children's learning through participation in performance-based experiences and the later viewing (via videotape) of those experiences. Both video footage and participant observation notes also indicated that through the collaborative nature of producing video performances, friendships within and across cultures were enhanced. A conceptual model for developing effective performance arts programming for children is presented, reflecting the importance of curriculum, training, and goal-oriented activities in facilitating optimal program outcomes. *[Article copies available for a fee from The Haworth Document Delivery Service: 1-800-HAWORTH. E-mail address: <getinfo@haworthpressinc.com> Website: <http://www.HaworthPress.com> © 2002 by The Haworth Press, Inc. All rights reserved.]*

KEYWORDS. Media, performance arts, cross-cultural friendships

INTRODUCTION

The present study grew out of an ongoing, "real life" summer program designed to positively affect the lives of urban children. While the potential harmful effects of the media have been discussed widely in recent years (Wilcox & Kunkel, 1996), media tools can be used for promoting positive socialization and healthy psychological development. Practice related investigations indicate that using video to enhance socialization skills, group cohesion and psychological development is effective with children and adolescents (Gardano, 1994). Additionally, contact theory research indicates that experiences where children have the opportunity to collaborate on projects with children of other cultures enhance multicultural understanding. These experiences promote the realization of similarities and help reduce the prevalence of stereotyped beliefs about individuals of different cultures (Slavin, 1985). For these reasons it was predicted that a program in which children collaborate across cultures producing videos would be effective for facilitating positive social and psychological outcomes. In order to evaluate this program's effectiveness, observations and interviews of children were conducted. In the process, a conceptual model for effective children's performing arts programming was developed.

Program Context

Children-produced videos have been used as part of the HOME (High-rise On-site Multi-family Environments) Family Support Program based in a diverse low-income neighborhood in Chicago.[1] The HOME program is an interdisciplinary program that is supported by a community/university partnership that facilitates effective programming and implements ecologically valid research. An urban subsidized high-rise has been the site of the HOME model program for 10 years. An important goal of this program is to use research findings to advocate for family support programming in other urban high-rise communities (Harding et al., 2001).

The urban community where the HOME program is housed is extremely diverse in terms of culture, ethnicity, and faith. The community is also poor and crowded. It has been found that living in a crowded environment may cause one to isolate one's self rather than seek out opportunities for socialization (Nyden, 1992). Resistance to socializing across cultures can negatively affect the sense of community within an urban high-rise as well as in the neighborhood at large. Additionally, stressors such as poverty, crime, domestic violence and lack of resources negatively impact hopes for the future and feelings of personal empowerment.

One of the primary guiding principles of the HOME program is to reflect a commitment to cultural diversity–encouraging families to live, play and work together. It is also the commitment of the HOME team to facilitate programming that meets with tenants' needs and requests. Tenants consistently expressed an interest in programming for children that enhances learning and skill development. Through writing, set design and construction, acting, directing and technical video operation, children of different cultures have opportunities for creative expression and skill development in the children-produced video project.

Summer 1997

In the summer of 1997, Video Production Club began as part of the HOME Family Support Program. The curriculum of this program provided opportunities for learning and creative expression. Participants between the ages of 6 and 15 years had opportunities to perform on video, and develop skills in script writing, set design and the use of video equipment. Curriculum and goals were determined in collaboration with participants. Facilitators included graduate and undergraduate university students in the areas of psychology, human development, and education. All program sessions were video-taped. Children also had frequent opportunities to view their taped performances.

This initial program offering served as an informal pilot study for program evaluation. Qualitative investigations from the first phase of the video project reflected the positive impact of the program. Field notes indicated that children enjoyed viewing their performances on video. The presence of the camera seemed to make the dramatic activities more interesting and meaningful. Children initially worked in groups based on prior friendships and similarity in gender, faith, and ethnicity. Later, as performances became larger in cast, some mixed gender, mixed culture groups performed collaboratively. These collaborations were different from those developed earlier. There was increased enthusiasm during these performances, increased excitement while viewing these performances, and an increased sense of camaraderie across cultural groups during the viewing of these performances.

Based on these early observations, specific program evaluation questions related to learning and friendship were posited for the present investigation:

1. Does a video arts program enhance learning?
2. How does a video arts program differ in its enhancement of learning from a non-video performance-based program?
3. Does a video production club enhance cross-cultural friendships?
4. How does video arts programming differ in its enhancement of cross-cultural friendships from a non-video performance-based program?
5. What factors contribute to programming outcomes for video and/or performing programming?

METHOD

Participants

HOME program participants from the summer of 1998 became participants in this exploratory study. Thirty-three children between the ages of 6 and 15 years old participated. One group of children (N = 15) were participants in the group using video (treatment); 19 participated in a similarly structured non-video group (comparison). Informed consent was obtained from the parent(s) or guardian(s) of each participating child.

Demographics. The population of residents living in the building as well as the community at large is diverse. Residents from this building include individuals of varying backgrounds who are US citizens as well as individuals and families from several different countries of origin. Volunteering children were randomly assigned from each cultural group so that the performance groups would have an equivalent cultural make-up. For specific demographics of the children who participated in this study see Table 1.

Procedures

During the summer of 1998, all children volunteering for the two performance-based clubs (the club with video and the club without video) were interviewed using a qualitative questionnaire which included questions investigating each child's expectations and interests related to the summer program and the child's openness to making new friends.

Throughout the program, trained research assistants who served as program facilitators maintained field notes regarding the children's affect, socialization, and behavior during programming. Facilitators documented the content of the session including a summary of the day's

TABLE 1. Participants

	Treatment (Video Group)	Comparison Group (Non-video Group)
Age		
6-7 years	4	4
8-9 years	6	6
10-12 years	3	4
13-16 years	1	5
Race/Ethnicity		
African/African-American	4	13 (3 from Ethiopia)
Pakistani/Indian/Nepalese	8	4
Vietnamese/Filipino	3	2
Gender		
Male	5	6
Female	10	13
N = (total children participating in programming)	15	19

program, problems or difficulties, each child's behavior and contribution, types of interactions and quality of interactions, any significant occurrences, and the facilitators' role using a semi-structured guide developed specifically for this study.

Children in the video group participated in theatre exercises, wrote scripts, created storyboards, performed plays, and practiced dramatic technique. Performances were videotaped at each session. Children spent the last 20 minutes of each session viewing their performances.

Children in the non-video group followed the same type of curriculum but performances were not taped and viewed. (For detailed curriculum information and training schedule please refer to Lynn, 1999.)

At the end of the summer of 1998, both program groups were interviewed using qualitative questions that examined friendships, skill development, and self-perceptions.

RESULTS

After completing field notes, research assistants/program facilitators rated each child on categories determined by group agreement. (Category definitions were determined by group agreement and relevant literature. Detailed information on rating and coding can be found in Lynn, 1999.) These categories formed an instrument developed for this study: the Child Rating Scale (Rai & Lynn, 1999). (Please see Appendix). After assessing overall instrument reliability using Cronbach's alpha, a score of .84 for this instrument was determined, indicating good overall instrument reliability for this assessment tool. Interrater reliability was assessed using Kendall's W (Tinsley & Weiss, 1975), a measure of concordance. The average coefficient for this rating scale was .84. The range of coefficients was .81 to .94.

Two outcome variables were measured: Quality of Cross-Cultural Interaction, and Learning. Other variables relevant to the topic are included in the following discussion. (A detailed discussion of all included variables can be found in Lynn, 1999.) The video group showed linear growth across the six sessions of the program. The non-video performance group showed more variability across all variables with trends toward linear growth starting at Sessions 3 and 4 for Learning and Quality of Cross-Cultural Interaction (see Figures 1-3).

FIGURE 1. Trends Analysis of Observed Learning

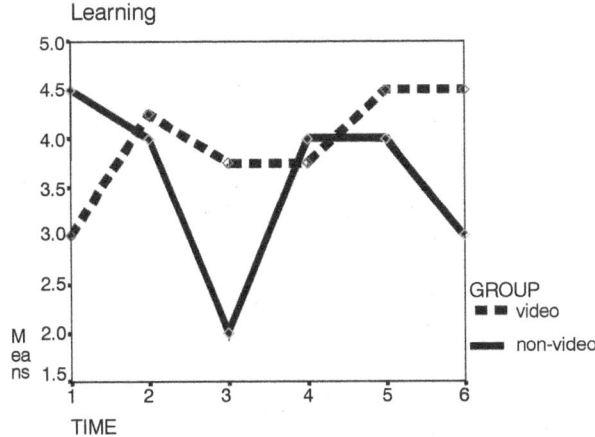

Note: Ratings for each category were based on a scale from 1-5, five being the highest possible score and 1 being the lowest. The above graph shows average group mean rating for the variable Learning across 6 program sessions.

FIGURE 2. Trends Analysis for Cross Cultural Quality Ratings

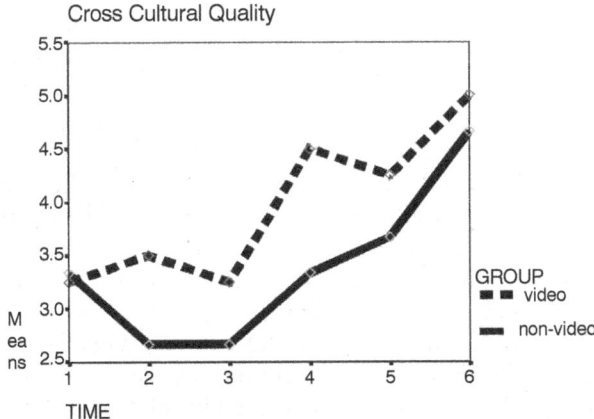

Note: Ratings for each category were based on a scale from 1-5, five being the highest possible score and 1 being the lowest. The above graph shows the average group mean rating for the variable Cross Cultural Quality across 6 program sessions.

FIGURE 3. Conceptual Model of Effective Community-Based Performing Arts Programming with Urban Children

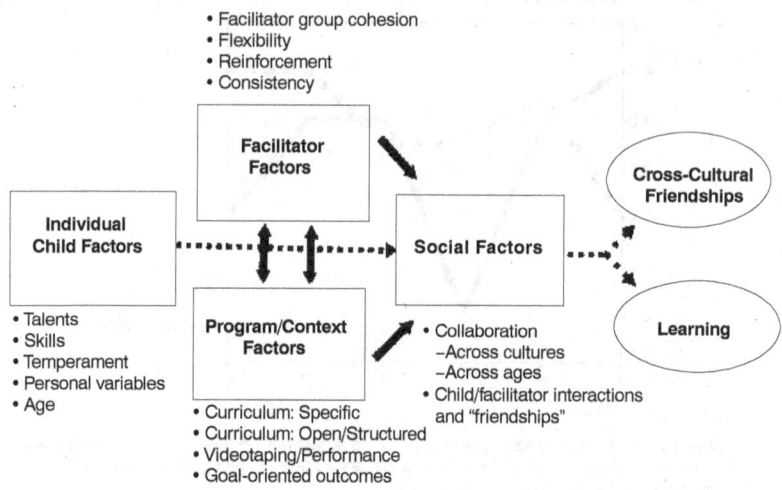

Conceptual Model for Programming

Facilitator field notes were also coded and analyzed in relation to the frequency of types of responses and quality of observed interactions and behaviors using a grounded theory method (Strauss & Corbin, 1990). An initial coding of facilitator field notes resulted in categorizing and sorting the data into themes. A more focused analysis of the codes and data resulted in the delineation of some specific concepts and relationships between these concepts. Qualitative results indicated that participation in the video production club and a non-video performance club promoted learning and cross-cultural friendships under certain conditions. Through this coding process (using both open and axial coding) a conceptual model for effective programming was determined. (See Figure 3). This coding process indicated that when certain factors were in place, outcomes were more optimal (as well as the reverse).

Within this model, factors are considered in relation to how they impact each other and how they affect cross-cultural friendships and indicators of learning. The four factors that emerged from the grounded theory coding process were (1) facilitation factors, (2) individual child factors, (3) program/context factors, and (4) social factors. *Facilitation factors* refer to the style of facilitation. Items in this category consist of cohesion among facilitators, flexibility, reinforcement/feedback, consistency, and redirection as appropriate. *Child factors* consist of what the child brings to the program. This factor includes temperament, culture, personality factors, talents, intellectual skills, experience and age. *Program factors* include components like the specific curriculum used, the use of video, open versus structured programming, goal oriented activities, and other program features (for example, performing for a block party sponsored by the building became a program goal and motivator during the summer of 1998). *Social factors* consist of social interactions that happen within the programs and include various types of collaboration between children as well as social interaction between the child and the adult facilitator. Session notes indicated the importance of cross-cultural collaboration and positive child/facilitator interaction for optimal outcomes. The schematic model depicted in Figure 3 provides a conceptualization of how all factors interact and contribute to learning and the development of cross-cultural friendships.

It is important to consider how this model can be employed in conceptualizing effective programming. As the model indicates, the child brings individual factors to the group and program/context conditions interact with these child factors affording opportunities for social factors (which include positive interaction within and across cultures). Consistent facilitation by trained facilitators contributes (through effective demonstration, reinforcement and redirection) to help create an environment with enough structure for optimal learning and friendly interaction. Through the opportunities, interactions, and curriculum these factors can afford and facilitate learning and cross-cultural friendships.

Child Self-Report Findings

Responses from participant interviews prior to and following programming were categorized into types of response. Findings from these interviews are summarized in Table 2. In general, the majority of children in both groups expressed an interest in skill development. An initial interest and later mastery in the area of social skill development were also commonly reported. The non-video group reported the development of performing arts skills more frequently at posttest. Both program groups also reported an interest in making new friends. Every child in both groups reported that "something had been learned" over the summer through participation in performance groups.

TABLE 2. Child Self-Report Findings

Responses	Video	Non-Video
Pretest		
Thought they would learn something new[1]	90.9% (n = 10)	91.6% (n = 11)
Expressed an interest in developing social skills[1]	63.7% (n = 7)	58.3% (n = 7)
Posttest		
Reported learning something new[2]	81.8% (n = 9)	69.2% (n = 9)
Reported social development skills[2]	45.4% (n = 5)	38.5% (n = 5)
Reported performing arts skills[2]	81.8% (n = 9)	30.8% (n = 4)
Reported talents in sports and academics*[2]	63.7% (n = 7)	Not Reported*
Reported less shy**[2]	Not Reported*	15.4%* (n = 2)
Reported making new friends[2]	63.7% (n = 7)	76.9% (n = 10)
Reported making other culture friends[2]	72.7% (n = 8)	61.5% (n = 8)
Reported believing they were talented[2]	100% (n = 11)	100% (n = 13)

Note: * Category based on open-ended response to "What are your talents?"

** Category based on open-ended response to "Did you learn anything new from this club?"

Response numbers are based on the number of children available for the pre- and post-test, not the number of children who signed up to participate in the club.

[1] pretest response

[2] posttest response

DISCUSSION OF FINDINGS

This study was primarily an exploration of how children's summer programming works from the perspective of trained program facilitators as well as from the perspectives of children themselves. Findings related to specific program evaluation questions are discussed below.

Does a video arts program enhance learning? While learning and mastery appear linear in the video group and fluctuate in the non-video group, both groups showed a positive trend after session two. Child self-reports also indicate increased learning for both groups. Most of the children reported an initial interest in learning and later reported that they felt they had developed specific skills.

Session notes indicated that children in the video group displayed positive affect during viewing and, in general, enjoyed performing. Some children in this program reported excitement early on to view their performances and remained excited throughout programming. Other children, while initially observed as apprehensive about performing and viewing, appeared to enjoy both activities by the third session. For some children the act of videotaping appeared to have a positive impact during the process and during the viewing of the tape.

How does a video arts program differ in its enhancement of learning from a non-video club? From various sources of data in areas related to learning, it can be concluded that the video group afforded more opportunities for positive affect and feelings of competence throughout the summer programming. However, by the end of the summer, both groups had opportunities for learning.

Does a video production club enhance cross-cultural friendships? For the video group, trends analysis indicated linear growth of cross-cultural friendships (see Figure 3). Session notes indicated cross-cultural collaboration for all children and task related camaraderie for all children who participated regularly. The development of cross-cultural camaraderie was evident among regularly attending females 7-9 years of age ($N = 6$). Based on these data it appears that this programming does foster cross-cultural friendship development.

How does video arts programming differ in its enhancement of cross-cultural friendships from a non-video performance-based program? Based on trends analysis, the non-video group showed linear growth of cross-cultural friendships after Time 3. Session notes indicated collaboration and task related camaraderie as of Time 3 which further improved in subsequent sessions. While children collaborated in the non-video group from the beginning, the quality of the collaboration for most children was lacking. Children participated as a group only for performances and planned independently for early sessions. Based on these data, it appears that while both programs demonstrated growth in the quality of cross-cultural friendships across time, the treatment group showed growth from the beginning and had a higher average occurrence of cross-cultural friendships (see Figure 3).

What factors contribute to programming outcomes for video and/or performing arts programming? The proposed conceptual model integrates the framework and tools necessary to facilitate learning and cross-cultural friendship development. It may serve as a guide to those who wish to implement or evaluate programming for children.

Findings from trends analysis illustrate the importance of video in creating both a goal-oriented activity that facilitates collaboration, as well as opportunities for learning experiences with immediate feedback. On the other hand, an interesting "real life" occurrence appeared to serve a similar purpose after Session 3 for the non-video group. The tenants' association began to plan a building-wide "block party." The task of "block party" preparation provided the necessary goals and structure to improve collaborations and opportunities for self-efficacy in the non-video comparison group. An interesting insight gleaned from this exploratory evaluation is the importance of the quality of goal-oriented activities necessary for both child enjoyment and positive social and developmental outcomes.

Other Factors Contributing to Program Outcomes

Facilitation. Findings from session notes as related to the conceptual model indicate that the role of facilitators is an important contributor to the effectiveness of these programs. Facilitators need to be able to knowledgeably lead group activities, effectively redirect behavioral problems, and remain flexible enough to work with the individual needs and interests of children of varying ages.

An interesting finding emerged from the children's interviews: younger children expressed a preference for and interest in adult volunteers. Qualitative questionnaires and session notes indicated that participating 6 year olds across groups had very positive attitudes toward adult facilitators. These children said they wanted to become friends with the facilitators or called them their friends.

Team Facilitation. Through the implementation of this summer program it became clear that working as a unified team of facilitators was crucial to program success. Facilitators for both groups met bi-weekly for training for three months prior to programming and then met weekly immediately after each program. This ensured that session facilitation went smoothly. Issues regarding program development and implementation were addressed as a group. Child behavioral issues and interventions were also discussed as a group and addressed immediately. Given the importance of adult input, knowledge, and flexibility, the lack of qualified volunteers or failure to provide ongoing training can be the downfall of many social service and community programs. Dedication and cohesion among facilitators for these programs were key to each program's ability to address behavioral issues, keep children's interest, and adapt programming based on children's talents and needs.

Mixed Age Programming. While diversity in age can cause problems for measurement in research, it can be argued that age diversity strengthens the programs by providing opportunities for mentorship by older children and opportunities for children just starting school to learn from their older peers. This kind of mixed age programming is consistent with Vygotsky's view of human development, specifically, Vygotsky's zone of proximal development (Vygotsky, 1978). The mentorship provided by teens and older children helped younger children to grasp concepts and engage in programming, while also motivating the older children and encouraging their learning. Although six year olds appeared to be confused and bored more easily and more likely to misbehave, it was also clear that they learned, developed, and contributed positively to their respective groups. Additionally, the key to the HOME project's success has been its inclusivity. All building children are encouraged to participate in HOME project programs. Any study within this project that limited participation to children of a limited age range would not reflect the true nature of inclusive programs such as the HOME project.

Limitations and Implications for Research and Programming

Most of the limitations of this study relate to limitations inherent to much of applied social research. Participants' attendance varied which affected both program implementation and evaluation. Cultural groupings were difficult to interpret. What distinguishes groups from an adult perspective is not necessarily the child's interpretation of who is or is not part of her/his group. In any programming for children, personality factors and behavioral difficulties from specific children can strongly impact program session success. For these reasons, a combined approach to assessment is essential in most applied social research studies. When evaluating and conducting research in real world settings, a mix of both qualitative and quantitative methodologies is essential for gaining greater understanding and clarifying contextual factors. Additionally, the use of participant observers is also essential. Researchers who know the children and have developed relationships with their families can better document and assess the children's interactions, affect, and behavior. While there are risks that come with familiarity (i.e., the loss of objectivity), this ecologically valid approach strengthens research conducted in real-life settings.

CONCLUSION

One reason for conducting this exploratory study was to provide evidence to support the importance of educational experiences in the arts for children. With threats of cuts of such programs from communities and public schools, it is important to demonstrate that children could be losing valuable opportunities not just to learn to act, sing, or dance, but also to learn about themselves, gain social skill development, and gain confidence and invaluable networks with peers across cultures. According to Pettigrew (1997), these relationships and positive feelings about individuals from other cultural groups can be generalized to help the individual have more openness towards other cultural groups with whom they are not familiar. Such possibilities make it clear that programs like these are necessary for the enhancement of intergroup relations. If children can develop common bonds and understandings with individuals of different cultures, they are more likely to develop into tolerant adults.

Similarly, programs that provide learning experiences for children are necessary to help children in low-income urban neighborhoods develop the sense of competency necessary to foster resilience given their environmental stressors. The positive developmental and social outcomes observed in this study and reported by the children themselves indicate the importance of innovative programming in urban family support programs. The conceptual model proposed can serve as a guide for developing programs that foster increased understanding, a sense of community, and a sense of personal efficacy, thereby helping children develop both as individuals and as members of the community.

NOTE

1. The HOME Family Support Program (under the direction of Carol Harding, PhD) has been supported by several funding sources, including the Helen V. Brach Foundation, Loyola University Chicago, and the Chicago Community Development Corporation.

REFERENCES

Fuerst, J.S. (1991). High-rise housing for low-income families. *Public Interest*, Summer.
Gardano, A. C. (1994). Creative video therapy with early adolescent girls in short-term treatment. *Journal of Child and Adolescent Group Therapy, 4* (2), 99-116.

Harding, C.G., Lynn, L.K., Sweatt, L., London, L., Reyes, R., Carter, P., & Rai, B. (2001, in revision for publication). The HOME Family Support Program: Guiding principles for working with people where they live.

Lynn, L. (1999). Children's Video Production in an Urban Family Support Program: Implications for Self-Efficacy and Cross-Cultural Friendships. Unpublished Dissertation, Loyola University Chicago.

Nyden, P. (1992). Our hope for the future: Youth family and diversity in the Edgewater and Uptown Communities. Report completed in cooperation with Organization of the NorthEast and funded by the Chicago Community Trust. Chicago.

Pettigrew, T. F. (1997). Generalized intergroup contact effects on prejudice. *Personality and Social Psychology, 23* (2), 173-175.

Rai, B., Lynn, L., McManus, S., & Kitcharoen, K. (1998). Child Rating Scale (Unpublished tool for rating child behavior and affect).

Slavin, R.E. (1985). Cooperative learning: Applying contact theory in desegregated schools. *Journal of Social Issues, 41* (3), 45-62.

Strauss, A., & Corbin, J. (1990). *Basics of Qualitative Research: Grounded Theory Procedures and Techniques.* Newbury Park, CA: Sage Publications.

Tinsley, H. & Weiss, D. (1975). Inter-rater reliability and agreement of subjective judgments. *Journal of Counseling Psychology, 22* (4), 358-376.

Vygotsky, L.S. (1978). *Mind in Society: The Development of Higher Psychological Processes.* Cambridge, MA: Harvard University Press.

Wilcox, B. & Kunkel, D. (1996). Taking television seriously, children and television policy. *Children, Families and Government,* 333-352.

APPENDIX

CHILD RATING SCALE
(Rai, B., Lynn, L., 1998)

Rate each child for each category on a scale from 1 to 5 (5 being the best). See definition sheet for category definitions.
N indicates where child's initials were inserted for coding.

Categories Scored	N	N	N	N	N	N	N	N	N	N	N	N
Uniqueness of Idea												
Worked Independ												
Worked Collab												
Idea Development Independent												
Idea Development Collaborative												
General Affect												
Resp to Praise												
Perform Affect												
Viewing [2] Self Affect												
Viewing[1] Other Affect												
Learning Evidence												
Child Sense of Mastery												
Behavior Uncoop/Coop												
Frequency X Cult												
Frequency S Cult												

X = Cross Culture S = Same Culture
Indicate present or not present for each variable below with a check (present) or a dash (not present). If unsure, leave blank.

X no inter												
X neg												
X utilitarian												
X collab												
X task related camaraderie												
X non related camaraderie												
S no inter												
S neg												
S utilitarian												
S collab												
S task related camaraderie												
S non related camaraderie												

---

[2] The child rating scale for comparison group # 1 (The Bomb) included the variable "Watching Others Affect" in place of both the viewing self and viewing others affect variables which relate to video viewing.

APPENDIX (continued)

CHILD RATING SCALE DEFINITIONS

*A-D indicate literature consulted in the development of definitions.

<u>Uniqueness of idea</u>: level of originality as observed during the planning process and performing. (A) (B)

<u>Worked collaboratively</u>: planned/ practiced/performed with others. Participated as part of a group.

<u>Worked independently</u>: planned and/or practiced/ performed alone

<u>Idea development independent</u>: planned ideas for performance's alone. (A)

<u>Idea development collaborative</u>: discussed ideas as part of a group/brainstorming. (A)

<u>General Affect</u>: observed mood (often seen in facial expression)

<u>Response to praise</u>: positive /negative as seen through verbalization and affect.

<u>Performing affect</u>: apparent mood while performing --uncomfortable/upset--happy/excited

<u>Watching others affect</u>: apparent mood while watching others perform --negative comments, negative teasing--happy, smiling positive laughter, positive comments.

<u>Viewing self affect</u>: apparent mood while viewing self on video ---uncomfortable/upset--happy/excited (as observed through verbalizations and facial expressions)

<u>Viewing others affect</u>: apparent mood while viewing others on video--negative comments, negative teasing--happy, smiling positive laughter, positive comments.

<u>Learning Evidence</u>: skill development/improvement--observed

<u>Child's sense of mastery</u> : Child's observed sense of skill development as perceived through willingness to repeat action and positive affect and verbalizations before/during /after action. (C)

<u>Behavior cooperative/uncooperative</u>: disruptive, disrespectful ignoring redirection, negative comments--listening to instructions, cooperating with adults and peers.

<u>Frequency of cross cultural interaction</u>: number of times child verbally/ physically associates with peer of another culture.

The following are related to both cross-cultural (X) and Same Culture (S) interactions.

<u>Camaraderie</u>-a spirit of friendly good fellowship indicated through shared enjoyment, shared enthusiasm, smiling, laughing, joking. (D)

<u>Task related camaraderie</u>: camaraderie as related to planning/ practicing/performing /viewing (D)

<u>Non task related camaraderie:</u> camaraderie unrelated to planning/practicing/performing/viewing (D)

<u>No interactions</u>: did not associate with peer of that cultural group.

<u>Utilitarian</u>: interactions as needed to complete tasks. Not friendly or unfriendly. ex: "We should do this....", "Hand me the poster board."

<u>Negative interaction</u>: isolating/alienating others. Making hurtful comments to others. Negative teasing, Arguing. Ignoring person when approached. Refusing to let person collaborate with him/her.The definitions were developed through facilitator/research team discussion and are based on consensus as well as relevant literature.

Child Rating Scale References

(A) Csikszentmihalvi, M. Creativity. New York, NY: Harper Collins Publishing.

(B) John-Steiner, V. <u>Notebooks of the Mind</u>. Albuquerque, New Mexico: University of New Mexico Press
(C) **Bandura, A.(1989). Social cognitive theory. <u>Annals of Child Development</u>, 6, 42-53.**
(D) Deegan, J. <u>Children's Friendships in Culturally Diverse Classrooms</u>. Gunpowder Square, London: The Falmer Press.

Kids' College: Enhancing Children's Appreciation and Acceptance of Cultural Diversity

Lorna H. London

Loyola University Chicago

Gregory Tierney

Northern Illinois University

Larisa Buhin
Dawn M. Greco
Christofer J. Cooper

Loyola University Chicago

SUMMARY. It is estimated that by the year 2010, African-Americans and Hispanic-Americans will no longer be considered an ethnic minority in our country. As our society moves toward greater cultural heterogeneity, children from diverse ethnic and cultural backgrounds will be interacting with one another on a larger scale in school, work, and play. This study explores the effects of the multicultural intervention program Kids' Col-

---

Address correspondence to: Lorna H. London, Family Practice Residency Program, Rush-Copley Medical Center, 2020 Ogden Avenue, Suite 325, Aurora, IL 60504.

The authors express appreciation to the Chicago Public Schools and the Board of Education for grant funding for this project.

[Haworth co-indexing entry note]: "Kids' College: Enhancing Children's Appreciation and Acceptance of Cultural Diversity." London, Lorna H. et al. Co-published simultaneously in *Journal of Prevention & Intervention in the Community* (The Haworth Press, Inc.) Vol. 24, No. 2, 2002, pp. 63-78; and: *Community Interventions to Create Change in Children* (ed: Lorna H. London) The Haworth Press, Inc., 2002, pp. 63-78. Single or multiple copies of this article are available for a fee from The Haworth Document Delivery Service [1-800-HAWORTH, 9:00 a.m. - 5:00 p.m. (EST). E-mail address: getinfo@haworthpressinc.com].

© 2002 by The Haworth Press, Inc. All rights reserved.

lege on children's self-esteem, ethnic pride, prejudice, and stereotyping attitudes. The 10-13-year-old children enrolled in the Kids' College program were the participants of the study. Kids' College is a six-week summer program designed to increase children's understanding of and appreciation for cultural diversity. A goal of the program is to decrease children's prejudices by providing an atmosphere where positive interpersonal relationships with children of different ethnic groups can develop. Participants of the study included 14 Caucasian, 35 African-American, 27 Asian, 26 Hispanic, and 11 multi-racial children.

Participants were given measures to assess their self-esteem, ethnic pride, multi-group prejudice, and stereotyping attitude. Results showed that general self-esteem increased at post-test ($M = 3.08$), $t(37) = 8.31, p = 0.00$ and across three subscales: school ($t(37) = 5.89$); home ($t(36) = 9.128$); and peer ($t(37) = 6.144$), $p = 0.00$ for all subscales. Multi-group prejudice significantly decreased at post-test ($M = 0.17$), $t(37) = 3.65, p = 0.00$. No significant differences from pre- to post-test were shown for ethnic pride. Implications for future research are discussed. *[Article copies available for a fee from The Haworth Document Delivery Service: 1-800-HAWORTH. E-mail address: <getinfo@haworthpressinc.com> Website: <http://www.HaworthPress.com> © 2002 by The Haworth Press, Inc. All rights reserved.]*

KEYWORDS. Prejudice, self-esteem, prevention, multicultural training

On July 4, 1999, 21-year-old Ben Smith went on a two day shooting spree through Illinois. All of his victims and others shot at but not injured were members of racial or religious minorities (Walsh, 1999). Earlier in August 1999, Buford Furrow, Jr., 37, shot five children at the North Valley Jewish Community Center in the San Fernando Valley. Also killed in the shooting was a Filipino-American mail carrier, Joseph Ileto. At the time of his arrest, Furrow stated that Ileto "was a good target of opportunity to kill because he was not white and worked for the federal government" ("Shooting Probe," 1999).

Such examples of racially-based violent acts illustrate little acceptance and appreciation of people from diverse racial and cultural backgrounds and further demonstrate a need for interventions designed to reduce prejudicial behaviors. Brown (1995) expanded Allport's (1954) definition of prejudice to "the holding of derogatory social attitudes or cognitive beliefs, the expression of negative affect, or the display of hostile or discriminatory behavior towards members of a group on account of their membership of that group" (Brown, 1995, p. 8). In order for children to relate well with one another in our increasingly diverse world, it is important that they learn about each other's background and work toward developing attitudes that foster an appreciation for people from diverse racial and cultural backgrounds.

Multicultural interventions that have been utilized in the past to increase children's acceptance of one another have often relied exclusively on self-report measures of attitudes, with no behavioral indices of attitudes (Bunton & Weisbach, 1974; Singh & Yancey, 1974; White & Sedlacek, 1987; Yawkey & Blackwell, 1974). One notable exception is the intervention work done by Clore, Bray, Itkin and Murphy (1978) which effectively incorporated behavioral indices of attitudes into the assessment.

Many multicultural interventions have been implemented in the school system (Damico, Bell-Nathaniel, & Green, 1980; Gumaer, 1973; Swadener, 1976; White & Sedlacek, 1987). Although it is important to target children in a place where they are easily accessible, these interventions may lack the intimate, friendly contact that is necessary for sustained attitude change. In addition, contact within the schools tends to be casual and not conducive to the establishment of close, personal interactions (Damico et al., 1980; Williams & Ryan, 1954).

Some interventions have applied a curriculum-based, educational approach (Rooney-Rebeck & Jason, 1986; Singh & Yancey, 1974; Slavin & Madden, 1979; Sleeter & Grant, 1987; Yawkey & Blackwell, 1974). Historically, curriculum-based programs suffer from two main design flaws. They often focus on teaching children about the holidays and customs of diverse racial and cultural groups thereby presenting only a limited view into the uniqueness of each culture. Also, they do not incorporate a developmental framework that can serve to encourage empathy and an increased level of social sensitivity.

Furthermore, curriculum-based programs often found in academic settings follow a hierarchical status system based on academic performance. Such a system leads to acceptance of racially and ethnically diverse children who are academically successful and rejection of academically unsuccessful children (Rist, 1978; St. John & Lewis, 1975) which in effect, further aggravates racial and social distancing in the classroom (Bossert, 1979; Damico et al., 1980).

A number of multicultural programs have been implemented in environments that are not multicultural themselves (Swadener, 1976). Such non-multicultural settings fail to model for the children the very behaviors and attitudes they are expected to foster. Similar programs are racially, culturally, and socially homogeneous, and do not allow for cross-racial interaction.

Singular focus in many programs is yet another problem (Singh & Yancey, 1974; White & Sedlacek, 1987). In such programs, the focus is solely on learning about one culture (i.e., Native-American, African-American, Hispanic, or Asian). In order to broaden the child's scope of the diversity of cultures, it is important to incorporate more than one culture into an intervention.

Multicultural interventions have also been designed in a summer camp format (Clore et al., 1978; Eaton & Clore, 1975). Behavioral and self-report measures were implemented at the start and at the end of such interventions to assess differences in children's attitudes. Positive results reported in children's attitudinal change are noteworthy and give credence to an intervention based on contact theory. However, a concern noted by the researchers was the danger of children's attitudes being temporary because the nature of the intervention was temporary.

Kids' College: A Kaleidoscope of Cultures is a multicultural intervention program whose premise is to counter the limitations of previous studies. The program is aimed at teaching children about people of other cultures through culture-specific dance, art, music, history, geography, and literature and, consequently, decreasing children's prejudicial attitudes and discriminatory behavior. The goals and objectives of the program are fourfold: (1) to reduce prejudice and stereotyping attitudes, (2) to increase knowledge about different cultures, (3) to increase cross-race friendships, and (4) to increase the child's self-esteem and own ethnic pride.

Kids' College is funded by a four-year grant from the local Board of Education, and represents a collaboration between a university in an urban community and the local public school system. This collaboration reflects the shared commitment of both organizations to intervene early with children before issues of prejudice and discrimination become a problem. By combining resources, areas of expertise, and shared vision, the Kids' College program has been able to attract inner-city youth and provide them with opportunities to expand their worldview and develop more accepting cultural attitudes and behaviors.

Kids' College is based primarily on Katz's theory of ethnic attitude formation, contact theory (Allport, 1954; Amir, 1969; Bullock, 1977; Kamal & Maruyama, 1990; Mann, 1959; Miller, 1990; Roper, 1990), and cooperative learning theory (Cosden & Haring, 1992; Davis, 1984; Johnson & Johnson, 1982; Johnson, Johnson, Tiffany, & Zaidman, 1984; Miller, Rogers, & Hennigan, 1983; Rzoska & Ward, 1991;

Weigel, Wiser, & Cook, 1975). These theories have been shown to affect attitude formation and attitude change. They also highlight the importance of frequent and varied opportunities to interact with culturally-different peers to facilitate the acquisition of accepting attitudes toward others. For these reasons, the Kids' College program was designed to include structures, activities, and conditions that are theoretically and empirically shown to be necessary for attitude and behavior change.

The Kids' College program is made up of six components based on contact theory and cooperative learning activities. The first component, *Games from Around the World,* involves an interactive game to establish close contact among the participants in a fun and friendly, non-competitive atmosphere. The games reflect activities that are played by children from different parts of the world.

My World Through My Eyes is the second component and introduces a guest speaker to guide the participants through each culture being studied. The speakers use a variety of teaching methods to introduce the children to their world. This interaction between speaker and participant provides an opportunity for participants to meet someone of a culture different from their own and can dispel myths about people from other cultures. Kids' College investigates six countries, or cultures, over the six-week term and invites guest speakers from each culture. In 1998, the program studied the following countries: Poland, Japan, Israel, Mexico, South Africa, and the United States of America. Many guests invited to speak were from the urban community and were affiliated with local consulates, cultural centers, speakers' bureaus, libraries, or international groups.

Cultural Cuisine is more commonly referred to as lunchtime, and is the third component of Kids' College. At this time children sample foods representing the different countries being studied. Lunchtime provides an opportunity for children to expel energy and interact in a fun way with their peers.

The fourth component is called *Classroom Creativity,* and involves a variety of group activities that give children an opportunity for cooperative interaction designed to achieve a particular goal. These cooperative activities involve all members of the group to participate and work together toward a common goal. During these activities, children participate in academic exercises and cooperative learning projects. Some projects are academic in nature, while others require children to utilize the creative arts to accomplish a stated goal.

KC Rap Session is the fifth component of Kids' College. During these sessions, children are encouraged to talk openly about personal experiences regarding prejudice and discrimination in an accepting and non-threatening atmosphere. Issues of self-esteem and conflict resolution are examples of topics discussed during these daily rap sessions. These discussions are facilitated by staff members, trained in basic counseling skills, and reflect diverse cultural backgrounds.

The sixth and final component involves a weekly field trip. These field trips are a chance for children to find diversity within their own greater community. For some, it represents the first time they have gone to a particular museum, festival, or visited another side of town.

Knowledge and contact alone are insufficient to change attitudes and behaviors and reduce prejudice (Allport, 1958; Bymes & Kiger, 1990). For this reason, Kids' College moves beyond just providing children with information and opportunities for casual contact with racially and ethnically diverse children. Kids' College gives children multicultural experiences and sustained cooperative contact in a friendly, non-competitive atmosphere. A variety of tasks are implemented in the program that requires teamwork, and there is no academic-evaluation component to foster competition. Based on recommendations from Clore et al. (1978), the Kids' College staff was comprised of individuals of different ethnic backgrounds who modeled positive relationships for the participating children.

Effects of the Kids' College intervention were examined with measures of self-esteem (i.e., school, home, and peer), ethnic attitude measures (i.e., ethnic pride and multi-intergroup prejudice), and stereotyping attitudes measure. It is hypothesized that there will be a difference in scores on self-esteem, stereotyping, and prejudice measures. It is also anticipated that a relationship will exist between self-esteem and prejudice.

METHOD

Participants

One hundred thirteen middle school children in fifth through eighth grades participated in the Kids' College program. Kids' College is a six-week summer program designed to increase knowledge of people of different cultures and decrease prejudice and discrimination through culture-specific art, dance, music, history, geography, and literature and cooperative learning activities.

Participants were students from several urban public schools and reflect the ethnic diversity found in this urban area. Students who scored at or above grade level on the Iowa Basic Skills test were eligible to join Kids' College. The sample was made up of 14 Caucasian, 35 African-American, 27 Asian, 26 Hispanic and 11 multi-racial children. These ethnic categorizations are based on the participant's ethnic self-identification from the Multi-Ethnic Intergroup Awareness Questionnaire.

Subjects were eliminated from the analysis if (a) data was missing on at least one of the measures used for this study and/or (b) individuals did not complete both pre- and post-measures. The final sample included 24 girls and 14 boys ranging in age from 10-13 years ($M = 11.68$). Participants completed measures assessing their self-esteem, ethnic pride, multi-ethnic group prejudices, and stereotyping attitudes. The distribution of children by race and gender is illustrated in Table 1.

Attempts were made to have equal representation of boys and girls from different racial groups in each of the five classrooms. The ratio of children to counselors per classroom was 5:1. Behavioral data was collected to examine friendship patterns. However, that data was not analyzed for this segment of the research.

Materials

Three assessments from archival pre- and post-test data collected from the 1998 Kids' College program were used for this study.

The Hare General and Area-Specific Self-Esteem Scale

The Hare General and Area-Specific Self-Esteem Scale (Hare, 1996) assesses an individual's school, home, and peer self-esteem and global self-esteem. The 30-item assessment contains three 10-item sections,

TABLE 1. Frequency Distribution of Participants, by Race and Gender (N = 38)

	RACE				
	Caucasian	African-American	Asian	Hispanic	Multiracial
Male	3	3	4	2	2
Female	5	9	4	5	1
Total	8	12	8	7	3

which assess school, home and peer self-esteem. Participants are asked to what extent they agree with a statement on a four-point Likert scale. Possible scores on the Hare range from 30 to 120. The Hare measure takes approximately 15-20 minutes to complete.

The Hare was found to correlate with the Coopersmith self-esteem schedule and the Rosenburg global self-esteem measure ($r = 0.83$). This high correlation provides substantial concurrent validity for the Hare. The Hare was also estimated to have a test-retest reliability 0.74 for the global self-esteem with this sample.

Multi-Ethnic Intergroup Awareness Questionnaire (MEIAQ)

The MEIAQ (Mahan & Bal, 1978) assesses ethnic pride, multi-ethnic prejudices, and ethnocentricity. Only the scores on ethnic pride and multi-ethnic intergroup prejudice were used for this study. An 18-item assessment, each statement on the MEIAQ reflects a personal characteristic, such as "are smart." Participants are asked to indicate how they feel about their own ethnic group and ethnic groups other than their own using a five-point Likert scale (e.g., all, most, some, few or none). To describe the level of prejudice on the MEIAQ, the authors created three categories for possible scores. Individual scores between 0.00 and 0.25 are considered unprejudiced; between 0.26 and 0.50 are considered somewhat prejudiced; and between 0.51 and 1.0 are considered highly prejudiced. This instrument has been used in other evaluations of multicultural educational programs (Mahan & Bal, 1978) and takes approximately 15-20 minutes to complete. The MEIAQ has not been psychometrically tested in previous research and therefore, information on its validity and reliability is not available.

Other People and Myself (OPAM)

The OPAM (McCormick & Kasnic, 1978) is a 10-item measure of acceptance and rejection of others from different backgrounds. Participants indicate to what extent they agree with certain stereotypes. The OPAM takes approximately 5-10 minutes to complete. Like the MEIAQ, this instrument has not been psychometrically tested in previous research, and, therefore, information on its reliability and validity is unavailable. However, own tests of internal consistency on the OPAM for this sample showed to be 0.32 ($n = 108$) at pre-test and 0.58 ($n = 76$) at post-test.

While scoring the assessments, three decision-rules were made to further preserve the sample population. First, when two answers were indicated for one question, the average of the two answers was used in calculating the score. Second, unanswered items were kept in the analysis by averaging the score of the completed items. Third, when calculating multi-ethnic prejudice in cases where a participant identifies with more than one ethnic group, scores were eliminated for all ethnicities with which the participant identified to deter scoring problems. These rules were constructed when decisions were not outlined in the testing manual.

Procedure

The Hare Self-Esteem measure, Multi-Ethnic Intergroup Awareness Questionnaire and Other People and Myself measure are paper-pencil tests administered in a group format. Participants completed these three measures at the beginning of the Kids' College program and again at the end of the six-week term. Graduate students administered the measures to the participants, who were instructed to respond independently and not share their answers with each other. Rather than using their names, participants were assigned an identification number to further ensure anonymity. All students voluntarily participated in this multi-cultural program, and written parental consent was obtained at the beginning of the program. The participants were informed from the start of the program that they may refuse to participate or withdraw from the program at any time without penalty.

Results

Analysis of all three measures showed no significant differences for either gender or ethnicity at pre- or post-test. An alpha level of 0.05 was used for all statistical analyses. However, analysis of the Multi-Ethnic Intergroup Awareness Questionnaire (MEIAQ) showed that multi-ethnic prejudice significantly decreased from pre-test ($M = 0.30$, $SD = 0.22$) to post-test ($M = 0.17$, $SD = 0.19$) with a $t(37) = 3.65$, $p = 0.00$ (see Figure 1). Paired sample t-test for the ethnic pride scale showed no significant differences from pre- ($M = 3.50$, $SD = 0.46$) to post-test ($M = 3.46$, $SD = 0.51$), $t(37) = 0.56$, $p = 0.58$ (see Figure 2).

Also using the paired sample t-test for analysis of the Hare Self-Esteem measure, general self-esteem significantly increased from the start ($M = 2.47$, $SD = 0.18$) of the six-week period to the end ($M = 3.08$, $SD =$

0.43), $t(37) = 8.31$, $p = 0.00$ (see Figure 3). Significant increases were also noted across the three self-esteem subscales. Table 2 presents the t-values across the subscales at pre- and post-test.

Paired samples t-test was used to analyze the data from the OPAM at pre-test ($M = 3.67$, $SD = 0.42$) and post-test ($M = 4.37$, $SD = 0.46$), $t(37) = 9.16$, $p = 0.00$ (see Figure 4). This finding indicates a significant increase in a belief in stereotypes.

FIGURE 1. Multi-Ethnic Prejudice: Pre-Test versus Post-Test

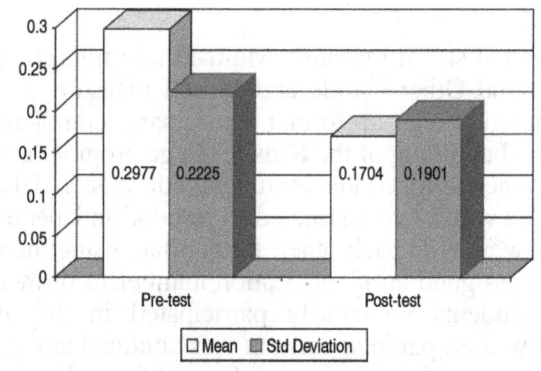

Note. Higher scores indicate higher levels of Multi-Ethnic Prejudice.

FIGURE 2. Ethnic Pride: Pre-Test versus Post-Test

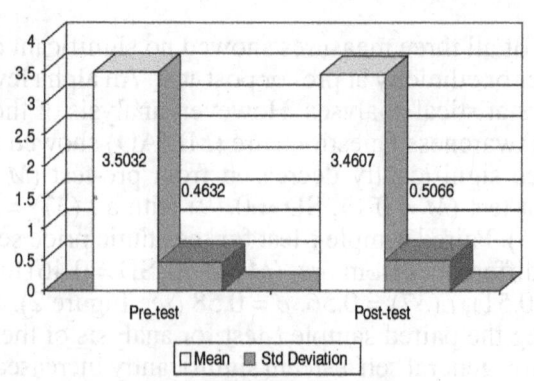

Note. Higher scores indicate higher levels of Ethnic Pride.

FIGURE 3. General Self-Esteem: Pre-Test versus Post-Test

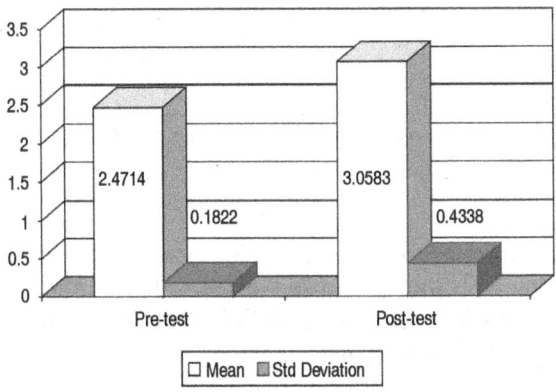

Note. Higher scores indicate higher levels of General Self-Esteem.

FIGURE 4. Endorsement of Stereotypes

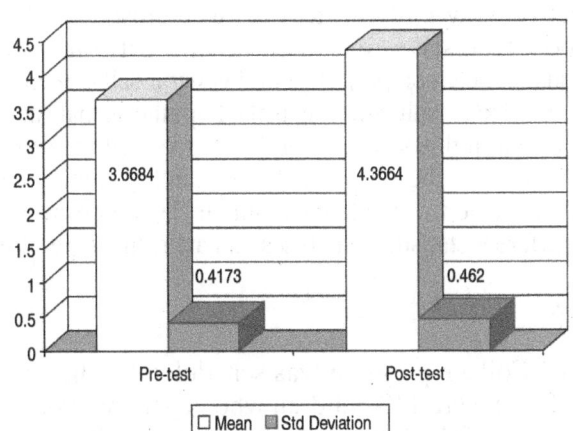

Note. Higher scores indicate higher levels of belief in stereotypes.

TABLE 2. T-Test Scores of Self-Esteem Subscales: Pre- to Post-Test

Self-esteem Subscale	t-values	Means	
		Pre	Post
School	5.885*	2.496	3.058
Home	9.128*	2.549	3.285
Peer	6.144*	2.378	2.847

Note. Degrees of freedom (df) = 37 with the exception of Home scale, df = 36.
*p = .000

Pearson Product Moment Correlation was used to determine a relationship between prejudice and self-esteem. It was shown that the relationship was not statistically significant at pre- ($r = -0.03, p = 0.86$) or post-test ($r = -0.20, p = 0.24$).

DISCUSSION

Although no significant differences were found for ethnicity, gender, or ethnic pride, further analyses of the measures lent some support of our hypotheses. The significant decrease of multi-ethnic prejudice from pre- to post-test indicates that participation in the Kids' College program may have had an effect on decreasing children's prejudicial attitudes. The overall increase of self-esteem of participants from before the intervention to after suggests that the Kids' College program has some effect on how children feel about themselves. Also, children's feelings about themselves increased in different contexts.

A relationship between prejudice and general self-esteem was not found for this sample. This result contradicts the hypothesis that such a relationship would be present in this study. Overall, the fact that the sample population was small can effect the power of the research findings. Also, numerous t-tests were conducted which tends to inflate Type I error. Reevaluating the data using different statistical analyses can avert this type of error.

Limitations

The Kids' College program was scheduled for the summer and was voluntary. There were 113 children who began the program. Of that total, 68 children finished the program. Several children were unable to complete the full six weeks because of vacation, illness, or prior commitments. Also, many children were absent on the day of post-testing. Therefore, the attrition of participants presented an obstacle for obtaining complete data. There were over five measures administered at the beginning and at the end of the Kids' College program. Despite efforts to spread out the measures over a couple days, children exhibited signs of dislike and exhaustion in having to complete the measures a second time. Also, some participants were returning students to the program who are familiar with goals of the program and the measures used for program assessment. Carryover effects and demand characteristics may have resulted from this familiarity with the program. These limitations may account for inaccuracy in measurement.

Furthermore, the limited use and insufficient statistical evidence on the reliability and validity of the Multi-Ethnic Intergroup Awareness Questionnaire and Other People and Myself measure are limitations to this study.

Implications for Further Research

The effect Kids' College had on children's self-esteem, ethnic pride, and multi-group prejudice scores may be generalizable to other children given the diverse make up of the sample group. Additional research must include a larger sample size. This may be achieved by establishing a control for attrition, such as charging a nominal fee for inclusion in the multi-cultural program. Also, a control group of children not involved in Kids' College could be included to determine the effects of the program. Follow-up interviews or self-report measures assessing ethnic pride, multi-group prejudice, and stereotyping attitudes of participants should be instituted a few weeks after completion of the program to evaluate any long-term effects of the program. In addition, a more systematic process for data collection needs to be established.

Conclusion

The Kids' College multicultural intervention appears to have a positive effect on children's self-esteem. This outcome supports the program's goal of increasing children's self-esteem.

While no significant difference was found in scores of ethnic pride, it may be important to clarify the concept of ethnic pride. It is possible that this variable is not well-defined, and thus may be difficult to measure. Additionally, because Kids' College stresses an appreciation for ethnic cultures other than the child's own, the program may want to include activities that require children to present information on their own cultural background in order to prevent any significant decreases in ethnic pride scores in the future. By involving children to share aspects of their culture with peers, they are also learning about their cultural heritage and growing in appreciation for their ethnic identity. A balance of ethnic self-pride and an appreciation for diversity would strengthen the goals of Kids' College.

Historically, participants of Kids' College have been volunteers from various ethnically diverse urban public schools. Conducting the Kids' College program with children reported to demonstrate prejudicial behavior or not generally in contact with culturally different children may better demonstrate the potential benefits of the intervention.

REFERENCES

Allport, G. W. (1954). *The Nature of Prejudice.* Reading, MA: Addison-Wesley.
Amir, Y. (1969). Contact hypothesis in ethnic relations. *Psychological Bulletin, 71*(5), 319-342.
Bossert, S. (1979). *Tasks and Social Relationships in Classrooms.* Cambridge, MA: Cambridge University Press.
Brown, R. (1995). *Prejudice: It's Social Psychology.* Oxford, UK: Blackwell Publishers, Ltd.
Bullock, C. S. (1977). Contact theory and racial tolerance among high school students. *School Review, 86,* 187-218.
Bunton, P. L. & Weissbach, T. A. (1974). Attitudes toward blackness of black preschool children attending community-controlled or public schools. *The Journal of Social Psychology, 92,* 53-59.
Byrnes, D. & Kiger, G. (1988). Ethical and pedagogical issues in the use of simulation activities in the classroom: Evaluating the "blue eyes-brown eyes" prejudice-reduction simulation. Utah State University (ERIC Document Reproduction Service No. ED 300 491).
Clore, G. L., Bray, R. M., Itkin, S. M., & Murphy, P. (1978). Interracial attitudes at a summer camp. *Journal of Personality and Social Psychology, 36*(2), 107-116.
Cosden, M. A. & Haring, T. G. (1992). Cooperative learning in the classroom: Contingencies, group interactions, and students with special needs. *Journal of Behavioral Education, 2*(1), 53-71.
Damico, S., Bell-Nathaniel, A., & Green, C. (1980). Effects of school organizational structure on interracial friendships in middle schools. *Journal of Educational Research, 74,* 388-393.
Davis, B. R. (1984). Evaluation of race/human relations program: A study of cooperative learning environment strategies. Unpublished manuscript.

Eaton, W. O. & Clore, G. L. (1975). Interracial imitation at a summer camp. *Journal of Personality and Social Psychology, 32*(6), 1099-1105.

Gumaer, J. (1973). Peer-facilitated groups. *Elementary School Guidance and Counseling, 8*, 4-11.

Hare, B. R. (1996). The Hare general and area specific (school, peer, and home) self-esteem scale. In R. L. Jones (Ed.), *Handbook of Tests and Measurements for Black Populations*. (pp. 199-206). Hampton, VA: Cobb & Henry.

Johnson, D. W. & Johnson, R. T. (1982). Effects of cooperative, competitive, and individualistic learning experiences on cross-ethnic interaction and friendships. *The Journal of Social Psychology, 118*, 47-58.

Johnson, D. W., Johnson, R. T., Tiffany, M., & Zaidman, B. (1984). Cross-ethnic relationships: The impact of intergroup cooperation and intergroup competition. *Journal of Educational Research, 78*(2), 75-79.

Kamal, A. A. & Maruyama, G. (1990). Cross-cultural contact and attitudes of Qatari students in the United States. *International Journal of Intercultural Relations, 14*, 123-134.

Katz, P. A. (1973). Stimulus predifferentiation and modification of children's racial attitudes. *Child Development, 44*, 232-237.

Mahan, J. & Bal, A. (1978). Measurement of interethnic intergroup perceptions of Youth Authority students. *Youth Authority Quarterly*, 1-43.

Mann, J. H. (1959). The effect of inter-racial contact on sociometric choices and perceptions. *The Journal of Social Psychology, 50*, 143-152.

McCormick & Kasnic. (1978). *Other people and myself*. Unpublished test.

Miller, N., Rogers, M., & Hennigan, K. (1983). Increasing interracial acceptance: Using cooperative games in desegregated elementary schools. *Applied Social Psychology Annual, 4*, 199-216.

Miller, R. L. (1990). Beyond contact theory: The impact of community affluence on integration efforts in five suburban high schools. *Youth and Society, 22*(1), 12-34.

Rist, R. (1978). *Invisible Children*. Cambridge, MA: Harvard University Press.

Rooney-Rebeck, P. & Jason, L. (1986). Prevention of prejudice in elementary school students. *Journal of Primary Prevention, 7*(2), 63-73.

Roper, P. (1990). Changing perceptions through contact. *Disability, Handicap and Society, 5*(3), 243-255.

Rzoska, K. M. & Ward, C. (1991). The effects of cooperative and competitive learning methods on the mathematics achievement, attitudes toward school, self-concepts and friendship choices of Maori, Pakeha and Samoan children. *New Zealand Journal of Psychology, 20*, 17-24.

Shooting probe in LA pursues hate-crime case. (1999, August 13). *The Chicago Tribune*, p. A1.

Singh, J. M. & Yancey, A. V. (1974). Racial attitudes in white first grade children. *The Journal of Educational Research, 67*(8), 370-372.

Slavin, R. & Madden, N. (1979). School practices that improve race relations. *American Educational Research Journal, 16*, 169-180.

Sleeter, C. E. & Grant, C. A. (1987). An analysis of multicultural education in the United States. *Harvard Educational Review, 57*(4), 421-444.

St. John, N. & Lewis, R. (1975). Race and the social structure of the elementary classroom. *Sociology of Education, 48*, 346-368.

Swadener, E. B. (1986). *Enhancing children's acceptance of diverse peers: Interaction patterns in two mainstreamed multicultural day care centers.* (Report No. 016867). University Park, PA: The Pennsylvania State University. (ERIC Document Reproduction Service No. ED 286 653).

Swadener, E. B. (1988). *Teaching toward peace and social responsibility in the early elementary years: A friends school case study.* Paper presented at the meeting of the American Educational Research Association Annual Meeting, New Orleans, LA.

Walsh, E. Racial slayer killed himself in struggle. (1999, July 6). *The Washington Post,* p. A1.

Weigel, R., Wiser, P., & Cook, S. (1975). The impact of cooperative learning experiences on cross-ethnic relations and attitudes. *Journal of Social Issues, 31*(1), 219-244.

White, T. J. & Sedlacek, W. E. (1987). White student attitudes toward blacks and Hispanics: Programming implications. *Journal of Multicultural Counseling & Development, 15*(4), 171-183.

Williams, R. M. & Ryan, M. W. (1954). *Schools in a Transition: Community Experiences in Desegregation.* Chapel Hill: University of North Carolina Press.

Yawkey, T. & Blackwell, J. (1974). Attitudes of four-year old urban black children toward themselves and whites based upon multiethnic social studies materials and experience. *Journal of Educational Research, 67*(8), 373-377.

Index

America's Promise Campaign, 4
Anxiety, 33, 34

BB/BS. *See* Big Brother, Big Sisters
Big Brother, Big Sisters (BB/BS)
   agency staff supervision, 11
   case example, 8-12
   as mentoring program, 7
   mentoring/youth matching practices, 10
Bracelet Behavior Program. *See* Incentive system, homeless youth summer camp

Child Behavior Checklist (CBCL), 36-37
Children's Action Tendencies Scale (CATS), 36
Community interventions. *See* Cultural diversity, acceptance of; Incentive system, homeless youth summer camp; Survival skills for urban youth; Video production, performance-based programming; Youth mentoring practices
Community psychologists, 1
Cross-cultural friendships. *See* Cultural diversity, acceptance of; Video production, performance-based programming
Cultural diversity, acceptance of, 2
   contact theory, 66,67

cooperative learning theory, 66
cross-race friendships, 66
ethnic attitude formation theory, 66
ethnic pride, 64,66,68,75-76
Kid's College program description, 64,66,67-68
multi-group prejudice, 64,68,71,72*table*,74
multi-group prejudice, measures, 70
multicultural interventions
   curriculum-based, 65
   non-multicultural environments, 65-66
   self report *vs.* behavioral measures, 65
   singular focus programs, 66
   summer camp format, 66
prejudice, defined, 64-65
prejudice reduction, 66
research discussion
   future research implications, 75
   limitations, 74-75
research method
   materials, 69-71
   participants, 68-69,69*table*
   procedure, 71
   results, 71-74
self-esteem, 64,66,68,71-72, 73*table*,74,74*table*,75
self-esteem, measures, 69-70
stereotyping attitude, 64,66,68,72,73*table*
stereotyping attitude, measures, 70-71
summary regarding, 63-64,75-76
youth violence examples, 64

Demographic Information Questionnaire, 36
Depression, 33,34
DuBois, David, 3

Ethnic pride, 64,66,68,75-76. *See also* Cultural diversity, acceptance of

The Handbook of School-Based Interventions (Cohen & Fish), 29
Hare General and Area-Specific Self-Esteem Scale, 69-70
HOME (High-rise On-site Multi-family Environments) Family Support Program, Chicago, 47
Homeless youth. *See* Incentive system, homeless youth summer camp
Hopelessness, 33,34
How My Child is Doing Survey (Nabors et al.), 20,24,28

Incentive system, homeless youth summer camp, 1
  behavioral problems, 17
  homeless statistics, 18
  mental health services accessibility, 17,18
  peer interaction problems, 17
  research limitations, 29-30
  research method
    behavior logs, 21-23
    data analysis, 23
    measures, 20
    participants, 19-20
    positive, negative behavior definitions, 22-23,22*table*
    procedure, 20-23
    program description, 19,20-21
  research results, 27
    behavior log analysis, 25-27, 26*table*
    bracelet program, 18,25
    discussion regarding, 27-30
    gender differences, 24-25, 24*table*,27-28
    parent perceptions, 24,28
    positive/negative behaviors, 26-27,26*table*
    teacher ratings, 24-27,24*table*
  summary regarding, 17-18,30
Isolation, 33,34

Kid's College. *See* Cultural diversity, acceptance of

Lynn, Laura Knight, 45

MEIAQ (Multi-Ethnic Intergroup Awareness Questionnaire), 70
Mentoring. *See* Youth mentoring
Mikalsen, Elena, 33
Multi-Ethnic Intergroup Awareness Questionnaire (MEIAQ), 70
Multi-group prejudice, 64,68,70,71,72*table,*74. *See also* Cultural diversity, acceptance of
Multiculturalism. *See* Cultural diversity, acceptance of; Video production, performance-based programming

Nabors, Laura, 17

OPAM measure (Other People and Myself), 70

Index

Other People and Myself (OPAM) measure, 70

Performance-based programming. *See* Video production, performance-based programming
Piers-Harris Self-Concept Scale, 37
Posttraumatic Stress Disorder (PSD) violence, exposure to, 33,34
Powell, Colin, 4
Project connect (PC) Summer Camp. *See* Incentive system, homeless youth summer camp

Self-esteem. *See also* Survival skills for urban youth
   cultural diversity acceptance, 64,66,68,70,71-72,73*table*, 74,74*table*,75
   goal setting, 9
   Kid's College cultural diversity program, 63-64
   validation of strengths, 8-9
   youth violence, 33,34,37,39, 39*table*,41
SOS! Help for Parents (Clark), 29
Summer camp. *See* Incentive system, homeless youth summer camp
Survival skills for urban youth
   coping skills, 1
   prevention programs, 34-35
   research discussion, 41-42
   research method
      measures, 36-37
      participants, 35-36
      program description, 36
      therapists, 37
   research results, 37-38
      age factors, 33,35,40,42

      behavioral symptoms, 38, 38*table*,41
      conflict resolution strategies, 38, 38*table*,41
      gender factors, 33,35,40, 40*table*,41-42
      main analyses, 38
      self-esteem, 33,35,37, 39,39*table*,41
   study limitations, 43
   summary regarding, 33
   victimization statistics, 34
Survival Skills program, University of Houston. *See* Survival skills for urban youth

Teacher Survey of Student Progress (Nabors et al.), 20

Urban youth. *See* Cultural diversity, acceptance of; Incentive system, homeless youth summer camp; Survival skills for urban youth; Video production, performance-based programming; Youth mentoring practices

Victimization. *See* Survival skills for urban youth
Video production, performance-based programming, 2
   group cohesion, 46
   multicultural understanding, 46
   program context, 47
   program history, 47-48
   psychological development, 46
   research discussion
      cross-cultural friendships, 46,55
      facilitator skills, 56

learning enhancement, 54-55
mixed age programming, 57
programming outcomes, 55-56
research implications, 57
research limitations, 57
team facilitation, 56
vs. non-video club, 55
research method
  Child Rating Scale, 50,60-61
  participants, 48-49
  procedures, 49-50, 49*table*
  program evaluation questions, 48
research results, 50-52
  child self-report findings, 53, 54*table*
  conceptual model for programming, 52-53,52*table*
  cross cultural friendships, 51*table*,52
  observed learning, 51*table*
  outcome variables, 50,51-52*tables*
socialization skills, 46,53
summary regarding, 45-46,58

Youth mentoring practices, 1,6
  academic adjustment, 9,10
  agency sponsored activities, 12,13
  agency staff supervision, 11,13
  barriers to, 9-10
  best-practices evaluation, 4*table*,5-6,13
  case example, 8-12
  effectiveness
    measurement of, 4
    suggestions regarding, 12-14
  goal setting, 9
  helping profession of mentor, 10-11
  increase in, 4
  literature review regarding, 4-6
  matching practices, 10
  mentor support group, 12
  participatory research, 6-8
    benefits of, 6,12
    meta-analysis benefits, 6
    quantitative *vs.* qualitative research, 6-7,14
  personal, environmental factors, 5,6
  relationship characteristics, 5,6
  summary regarding, 3-4,12-14
  validation of strengths, 8-9
Youth Self-Report (YSR), 37
Youth violence, 64